The Psychology of Graphic Design Pricing

Price creative work with confidence.
Win more bids. Make more money.

Michael Janda

The Psychology of Graphic Design Pricing:
Price creative work with confidence. Win more bids. Make more money.
By Michael Janda

www.michaeljanda.com
To report errors, please send a note to me@michaeljanda.com

Design: Michael Janda
Editor: Jodi Janda

9 8 7 6 5 4 3 2 1

Made in the United States of America

This book is dedicated to all of the freelancers, designers, and agency entrepreneurs who are tired of pulling pricing numbers out of thin air, hoping to make a profit.

ix Introduction

01/ 1 The Pricing Spectrum

02/ 5 Graphic Design and Profitability

03/ 8 Variable 01: Production Cost

9 Calculating Your Hourly Burn Rate

10 Scenario 01: Calculating Your Hourly Burn Rate Based on Annual Salary

12 Scenario 01: Worksheet

14 Scenario 02: Calculating Your Hourly Burn Rate Based on Personal Overhead and Freelance Business Expenses

15 Accounting for Taxes

16 Billable Time Available

19 Scenario 02: Worksheet

26 Scenario 03: Calculating Your Hourly Burn Rate Based on Agency Overhead Expenses

35 Scenario 03: Worksheet

42 Calculating Estimated Production Hours for a Project

47 Calculating Production Cost

52 Variable 01: Production Cost Worksheet

04/ 59 **Variable 02: Market Value**

61 Market Value Based on Return on Investment (ROI)

62 Market Value Based on Competition

62 Survey Your Clients

64 Review Industry Surveys

65 Leverage Your Experience

67 Establishing Market Value

69 Variable 02: Market Value Worksheet

05/ 75 **Variable 03: Client Budget**

77 How to Extract a Client's Budget

77 Ask the Client

79 Poker Face

80 Ask About Past Projects

80 Float a Price Range

82 Compare other Products

82 Send a Rough Estimate

83 Example Budget Extraction Conversation

85 How to Encourage Clients to Increase Their Budget

86 Discuss Money with Confidence

86 Educate the Client with Your Expertise

90 Price Anchoring

93 Provide the Client with a Range of Options

95 Create Doubt in a Competitor's Ability to Execute

96 Don't Play Games

97 Variable 03: Client Budget Worksheet

06/ 105 Creating the Pricing Spectrum

105 Take Time to Get Your Numbers Right

105 Organize Your Numbers from High to Low

106 Choose Your Price from the Spectrum

07/ 108 The Psychology of Choosing a Price

108 The Left-digit Effect vs. Whole Number Prices

113 12 Pricing Spectrum Scenarios

114 Scenario 01: Desperate for Work

116 Scenario 02: Yes, for the Right Price

118 Scenario 03: Slammed but Ambitious

120 Scenario 04: Difficult Client

122 Scenario 05: Experience Merits Money

124 Scenario 06: Trying to Grow

126 Scenario 07: Heavy Competition

128 Scenario 08: Budget too Low

130 Scenario 09: Big Budget

132 Scenario 10: Saving a Relationship

134 Scenario 11: Production Cost too High

138 Scenario 12: Creative Superhero

140 Pricing Spectrum Worksheet Sample

149 Blank Pricing Spectrum Worksheets

08/ 165 Calculating Your Billable Hourly Rate

165 Trading Time for Money Penalizes You
166 A Method to the Hourly Madness
169 Billable Hourly Rate Formula
173 A Final Warning
174 Billable Hourly Rate Worksheet

09/ 179 Pricing Presentation Strategies

179 Don't Just Email Pricing Numbers, Present Them
179 Commas and Pricing
180 Itemize Prices by Phases, Not Deliverables
184 Use Font Sizes Wisely
186 Solution First and Price Second
187 Show Your Discounts

10/ 191 Conclusion & Pricing Rules

192 Pricing Rules & Reminders for Graphic Designers

194 About the Author

*

When it comes to pricing their work, most designers are just pulling numbers out of thin air, hoping to make a profit.

Introduction

Have you ever sat in awe at the agency veteran who seems to know the client's budget as soon as they sit down at the table? Or the one who seems to know exactly what their competitors are charging? How about the one who can tell you, without even looking at the specs, what their agency will cost to produce a certain project? My goal is to help you become this person by teaching you to think like an agency veteran, to understand what goes on in their head when they analyze a particular client opportunity.

Unfortunately, there are far too many designers who don't "get it" when it comes to pricing projects. Over the past 20+ years, I have freelanced, owned an agency, managed hundreds of designers, overseen thousands of projects, and outsourced to countless freelancers; one thing is for certain, when it comes to pricing work, most designers are just pulling numbers out of thin air, hoping to make a profit.

The average designer says, "What should I charge for this? Um, well, how about $XXX? Ya, that sounds good. I'll charge that." Then they throw the number onto a rudimentary proposal and send it off to the client with fingers crossed, hoping for an approval.

This isn't just true with freelance designers, it is true with a lot of agencies as well. For half of the 15 years running my agency, I was using my "sixth sense" to guess on pricing in a quest to be the winning bid. I know of agencies that bill millions each year that do little more than guess at what they should charge.

Chances are that many of you do the same. Guess a price. Paste it on a proposal document. Send it to your client and hope for the best. All of this is about to change as I show you a methodical way to determine pricing for creative services so you can win more bids and earn more profit.

This is dense information, but if you learn these principles and apply them, it will be a game changer for you. Stick with me!

01

CHAPTER 01

The Pricing Spectrum

The reality of pricing graphic design is that some "guesswork" is involved. I'm not advocating guessing between charging $500 or $50,000 for a project. I am talking about that very final proposal number is oftentimes a "best guess."

What price do you place on your proposal? Will your client green light your project at $1,900? Would they still green light at $2,200? If your competition is charging $2,500, can you win the project by charging $2,400 or do you need to be at $2,300 to earn the business? Can you even make a profit at $2,300? Are you leaving money on the table if your price is too low? Are you losing bids because your price is too high?

In this book, I will teach you how to make a conscious decision about where to price your work based upon a careful analysis of three variables. First, you must understand your **cost to produce the work**. Next, you should take into consideration the **market value** for the work you are doing. Third, I will teach you how to discover your **client's budget**.

These three variables are used to create a low to high pricing spectrum from which you can intentionally decide where to price your projects.

This is a systematic method for pricing graphic design work and the corresponding analysis will help you choose the right price for every opportunity. I can't wait to show you how it works.

The Three Variables of the Pricing Spectrum

---

01 Production Cost

Your cost to produce the work your client is requesting.

02 Market Value

The fair market value for the work based on what other people like you are charging.

03 Client Budget

The amount of money the client has allocated to pay for the work.

*

Are you leaving money on the table when your price is too low? Are you losing bids because your price is too high?

02

CHAPTER 02

Graphic Design and Profitability

Before we dig into analyzing the three pricing variables, it is important to discuss the goal of pricing your work. Most artists who choose graphic design as a career path do so because it is one of the few types of "art" that offers consistent employment. Graphic design both scratches our artistic itch and allows us to pay the bills. As such, you should never feel bad about making money doing design work just because you love to do it. When you are pricing your work, you are looking to make a financial profit. The amount of profit varies from project to project, but never forget, **profitability is the goal**.

If you want to work for "free," then pick some pet projects and be your own client. If you are being hired by someone to do graphic design, then run it like a business and structure the agreement to ensure profitability.

Imagine your client approaches you with a project opportunity and asks for a bid. Excitement fills your soul as you can once again envision a future with bills paid and food on the table. Whew, that was a tight month! You analyze the project specifications and begin crafting a proposal. Undoubtedly, one of the first questions you ask yourself is, "How much should I charge?" Stop asking this question and rephrase it: "How much profit should I include in my price?"

The first step toward profitability is understanding your cost to produce the work.

*

Stop asking yourself, “How much should I charge?” and start asking, “How much profit should I include in my price?”

03

CHAPTER 03

Variable 01: Production Cost

If you have no clue how much it costs you to be in business, you are not alone. Most freelancers, and far too many agencies, don't understand their cost to be in business or produce work. For the agencies that don't understand their numbers, profitable projects are as frequent as unprofitable projects, and ending the year with a positive balance sheet has as much to do with luck as it does anything else. To say it nicely, creative people often struggle with analytical things.

This may sound obvious, but you should never take on a project that is guaranteed to be unprofitable. Unfortunately, freelancers and agencies do it all the time! They convince themselves that they are better off having some income rather than no income, so they cut deals for their clients to win projects. The sad truth is that this behavior changes their client's pricing expectations which perpetuates cutting deals on the next project, and the next. Before you know it, these ramen-noodle-eating designers or stressed out agency owners are five projects deep into an unprofitable client relationship and unable to pay their bills. Sound familiar?

You cannot consistently price projects profitably if you don't know your cost to produce the work.

Your production cost is the time it takes to do the work multiplied by your hourly cost (or hourly burn rate) plus any hard costs.

Understanding your cost to produce a project is critical to generating a profit and is not very difficult to determine. Your estimated production cost is your hourly cost (or your hourly burn rate) multiplied by the time it takes to do the work (estimated production hours); then, add any hard costs required to complete the project. I'll explain how to understand and calculate all of these items in the coming pages.

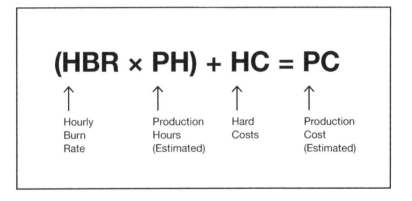

$$(HBR \times PH) + HC = PC$$

HBR ↑	PH ↑	HC ↑	PC ↑
Hourly Burn Rate	Production Hours (Estimated)	Hard Costs	Production Cost (Estimated)

Calculating Your Hourly Burn Rate

In order to understand your production cost for a project, you must first understand your "hourly burn rate," which is your hourly cost to be in business, or the rate you figuratively "burn money" each hour. Let's explore this in more detail by digging into a few different scenarios.

Scenario 01: Calculating Your Hourly Burn Rate Based on Annual Salary

Let's say you are a part time freelancer. Perhaps you work a full-time job and freelance on the side. Maybe your spouse works full-time and you freelance to generate some extra income for your family. Or perhaps you are just getting started in your career, still living at home with your parents, trying to get a little freelance career started. If any of these descriptions sound like you, then you are a great candidate for the easiest way to calculate your hourly burn rate.

To get started, simply take the annual salary that you feel you are worth and divide by 2,080. Where does the 2,080 come from? It is the business standard for full-time employment hours worked in a year. 2,080 is equivalent to working 40 hours per week for 52 weeks. Dividing your annual salary by 2,080 to calculate your hourly burn rate isn't perfectly accurate as it doesn't take into consideration paid time off or other costs, but it is an easy way to come up with an hourly rate. Here are a few examples:

If your market value salary is $48,000 per year, then divide it by 2,080 to yield a burn rate of $23.08 per hour.

Are you worth $60,000 per year? Divide it by 2,080 to yield $28.85 per hour.

$100,000 per year? Divide by 2,080 to yield $48.08 per hour.

This is the simplest way to calculate your cost per hour. It is sufficient enough for many part-time designers but lacks the accuracy that a business requires (which will be explained in the next two scenarios).

The following chart shows the calculation of hourly burn rates based on annual salaries ranging from $25,000 to $150,000 per year.

You will notice a column at the far right that shows the hourly burn rate rounded up. To simplify your calculations and to make your hourly burn rate easier to remember, I recommend rounding up your hourly burn rate to the nearest dollar. We round up, even if "math rules" say otherwise, because it is always better to err on the side of more profit, rather than less.

Annual Salary	Annual Production Hours	Hourly Burn Rate	HBR Rounded Up
$150,000	2,080	$72.12	$73
$145,000	2,080	$69.71	$70
$140,000	2,080	$67.31	$68
$135,000	2,080	$64.90	$65
$130,000	2,080	$62.50	$63
$125,000	2,080	$60.10	$61
$120,000	2,080	$57.69	$58
$115,000	2,080	$55.29	$56
$110,000	2,080	$52.88	$53
$100,000	2,080	$48.08	$49
$95,000	2,080	$45.67	$46
$90,000	2,080	$43.27	$44
$85,000	2,080	$40.87	$41
$80,000	2,080	$38.46	$39
$75,000	2,080	$36.06	$37
$70,000	2,080	$33.65	$34
$65,000	2,080	$31.25	$32
$60,000	2,080	$28.85	$29
$55,000	2,080	$26.44	$27
$50,000	2,080	$24.04	$25
$45,000	2,080	$21.63	$22
$40,000	2,080	$19.23	$20
$35,000	2,080	$16.83	$17
$30,000	2,080	$14.42	$15
$25,000	2,080	$12.02	$13

Hourly Burn Rate Scenario 01 Worksheet

Calculating Your Hourly Burn Rate Based on Annual Salary

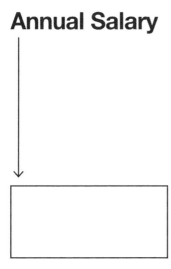

Annual Salary

Enter the annual salary you are worth in the marketplace.

÷ 2,080

Now divide by 2,080 (the estimated number of full-time work hours per year).

This is your hourly burn rate. If you bill 40 hours per week for a year, you will earn your annual salary.

Hourly Burn Rate

Scenario 02: Calculating Your Hourly Burn Rate Based on Personal Overhead and Freelance Business Expenses

A more accurate way to determine your hourly burn rate is based upon the actual costs to run your freelance business, combined with your personal overhead expenses. Although this method takes a little more time to calculate, it is far more accurate than picking a salary and doing the calculation described in Scenario 01. I recommend this method for people who are using freelance work as their primary source of income. However, even part-time freelancers can use this method to gain an exact view of their cost to do business.

Assume you are a freelancer working from your home. You are married with two children and your spouse doesn't work. Your freelance business is the primary source of income for the family. Begin by writing down all of your monthly expense categories. Include everything you need to spend money on in both your personal life and your freelance business. I've listed some common categories to help you get started.

- **Housing** (rent or mortgage payment)
- **Utilities** (water, gas, electric, internet access)
- **Health Care** (health insurance and monthly medical costs)
- **Transportation** (car payment, fuel, auto insurance, public transportation passes)
- **Food** (dining out and groceries)
- **Entertainment** (vacations, movies, streaming services)
- **Consumer Debt** (student loan payments, credit card payments)
- **Marketing and Advertising** (business networking, trade shows, social/traditional ads, website hosting, Pay Per Click advertising)
- **Business Expenses** (accountant fees, computer equipment, office supplies, business insurance)
- **Other** (Did you miss anything? Pet food? Shoe addiction? Tanning bed? Guitar lessons? Gym membership?)

Next, identify your monthly cost for each of these items and add them up to unveil your total monthly expenses. Let's look at how this might look for you, our full-time freelancer.

Budget Category	Monthly Overhead Expenses
Housing	$1,800
Utilities	$500
Health Care	$1,200
Transportation	$400
Food	$900
Entertainment	$300
Consumer Debt Payments	$300
Marketing & Advertising	$500
Business Expenses	$200
Other	$100
TOTAL MONTHLY EXPENSES	$6,200

Based on these expenditures, you have a $6,200 per month cost of living. If you make $6,100 in a month, you are losing money. If you make $6,300 in a month you have $100 of profit to save or spend on what you choose.

Now, take the $6,200 of monthly expenses and multiply it by 12 months to give you a personal annual expenses of $74,400.

Accounting for Taxes

There is one budget category that often goes overlooked: taxes. Depending on your income, your tax rate in the United States can range from 10% to 39.6%. Other countries have a wide range of income tax structures that may be different from that range. Let's just assume you will have some tax obligation to the government in which you live and for the sake of easy math, let's use 30% as our "tax budget" line item.

If you need $74,400 of income to cover your annual expenses, it will require an additional $22,320 to cover your taxes on that income. (This calculation is made by multiplying $74,400 by 0.30. If your anticipated tax rate is 20%, you would multiply by 0.20. Multiply by 0.15 for a 15% tax rate, and so on.)

Next, add the tax budget ($22,320) to the income you need for your annual expenses ($74,400); this equals the revenue needed to cover your total annual expenses with taxes ($96,720). In other words, you will need to earn $96,720 annually to pay for your personal overhead and freelancer business costs.

The calculation to arrive at your hourly rate is the same as in Scenario 01, divide by 2,080. Simply take your total annual expenses (including your tax budget) of $96,720 and divide by 2,080 (the number of full-time work hours per year). This calculation yields an hourly burn rate of $46.50. This is your "break-even" cost per hour. If you only charge this hourly rate and only bill for 2,080 hours per year, you will have nothing leftover at the end of the year. (We'll discuss ensuring profitability later in this book. For now, we just need an understanding of your cost to produce work for your clients.)

Billable Time Available

Now that we have all that figured out based on 2,080 hours per work year, let's get really crazy. Is it actually 2,080 hours? Are you really working 40 hours per week and 52 weeks per year? What about vacation? Holidays? A few sick days? What about the time that you spend doing things that you cannot bill to your clients?

When I was a full-time freelancer, I spent at least 25% of my time doing administrative things that I couldn't bill to my clients. These tasks include invoicing, accounting, networking, sales, marketing, running errands, and a variety of other necessary tasks to keep my business going. These hours are not billable to a client.

In this situation, I either needed to work 25% more hours per week OR calculate my hourly burn rate based upon 25% less time than 2,080. You will probably do the former and must do the latter (especially when you consider taking some holidays off and a vacation or two each year).

The grid below shows the work hours per year if you reduce them by 5% increments. The first column shows our 40 hours per week and 52 weeks per year number of 2,080. The next column shows the percentage of time you have available for billable work. The final column shows the actual number of billable production hours you have available per year adjusted by the billable percentage.

Annual Production Hours	Billable Percentage	Adjusted Annual Production Hours
2,080	100%	2,080
2,080	95%	1,976
2,080	90%	1,872
2,080	85%	1,768
2,080	80%	1,664
2,080	75%	1,560
2,080	70%	1,456
2,080	65%	1,352
2,080	60%	1,248
2,080	55%	1,144
2,080	50%	1,040
2,080	45%	936
2,080	40%	832
2,080	35%	728
2,080	30%	624
2,080	25%	520
2,080	20%	416
2,080	15%	312
2,080	10%	208

2,080	5%	104
2,080	0%	0

Let's look at a few calculation examples using our previously calculated expenses and this table. Knowing you need $96,720 to cover your personal annual expenses and assuming that you spend 25% of your year doing "non-billable" things, then you really only have 1,560 billable hours (75% of 2,080) available to generate the $96,720.

Annual Production Hours	Billable Percentage	Adjusted Annual Production Hours
2,080	75%	1,560

Therefore, you will divide $96,720 by 1,560 hours (instead of 2,080) to yield an hourly burn rate of $62 per hour.

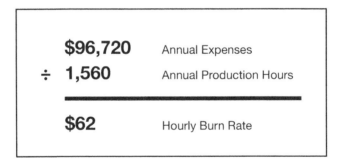

	$96,720	Annual Expenses
÷	**1,560**	Annual Production Hours
	$62	Hourly Burn Rate

All of this may seem a bit complicated, but it really is pretty straightforward once you dig in. I have provided a step by step worksheet to help you get organized and calculate your hourly burn rate using these formulas.

Hourly Burn Rate Scenario 02 Worksheet

Calculating Your Hourly Burn Rate Based on Personal Overhead and Freelance Business Expenses

Step 01:

Enter the monthly expenses for both your personal life as well as any costs for your freelance business and then add up the total. Your goal is to discover all the costs you have to run your life.

Budget Category	Monthly Overhead Expenses
Housing	
Utilities	
Health Care	
Transportation	
Food	
Entertainment	
Consumer Debt Payments	
Marketing & Advertising	
Business Expenses	
Other	
TOTAL MONTHLY EXPENSES	$

Step 02:

Take your total monthly expenses from Step 01 and multiply by twelve (for twelve months in a year). This calculation will unveil your annual expenses.

Total Monthly Expenses		**Annual Expenses**
$	**× 12 =**	$

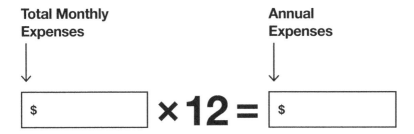

Step 03:

Take your annual expenses number from Step 02 and calculate the amount you will owe for taxes after you earn enough to cover your annual expenses.

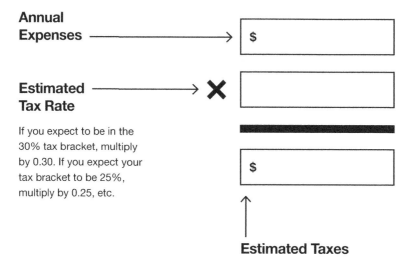

Annual Expenses → $

Estimated Tax Rate → ×

If you expect to be in the 30% tax bracket, multiply by 0.30. If you expect your tax bracket to be 25%, multiply by 0.25, etc.

$

↑

Estimated Taxes

Step 04:

Add your estimated taxes calculated in Step 03 to the annual expenses calculated in Step 02 to unveil your total annual expenses (with taxes).

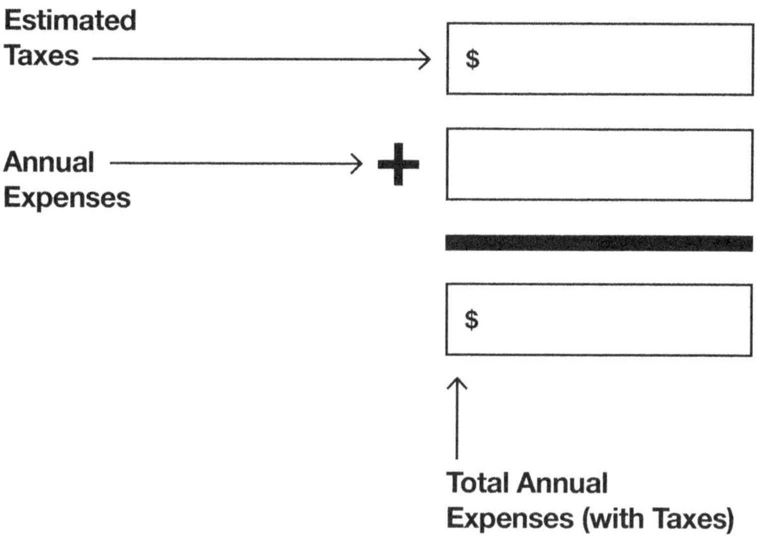

Step 05:

Using the chart below, determine your adjusted annual production hours based on how much time you actually have available for billable work. For example, if you are only able to spend 75% of your time doing tasks that you can bill to your clients, then your adjusted annual production hours are 1,560. (In other words, you spend 25% of your time in "non-billable" activities like vacations, errands, marketing your business and so forth.) If you are only able to spend 30% of your time on billable tasks, then you would have 624 annual production hours.

Annual Production Hours	Billable Percentage	Adjusted Annual Production Hours
2,080	100%	2,080
2,080	95%	1,976
2,080	90%	1,872
2,080	85%	1,768
2,080	80%	1,664
2,080	75%	1,560
2,080	70%	1,456
2,080	65%	1,352
2,080	60%	1,248
2,080	55%	1,144
2,080	50%	1,040
2,080	45%	936
2,080	40%	832
2,080	35%	728
2,080	30%	624
2,080	25%	520
2,080	20%	416
2,080	15%	312
2,080	10%	208
2,080	5%	104
2,080	0%	0

Step 06:

Calculate your hourly burn rate by dividing your total annual expenses (with taxes) from Step 04 by your adjusted annual production hours from Step 05.

Total Annual Expenses (with Taxes) → $

Adjusted Annual Production Hours → ÷

Use the chart in Step 05. (For example, if you spend 30% of your time each week doing "non-billable" activities and only 70% of your time is available for billable work, you would enter 1,456 in this box.)

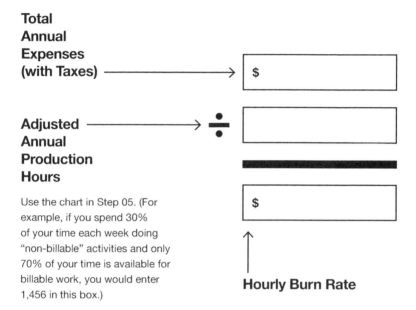

$

Hourly Burn Rate

Scenario 03: Calculating Your Hourly Burn Rate Based on Agency Overhead Expenses

I'll never forget the feeling I had when my agency expenses first exceeded $100,000 per month. It was about four years after the creation of my company and the feeling was a mix of awe and panic, but mostly panic. Burning through $25,000 per week took a little getting used to (and that was just the start of bigger expense numbers that increased exponentially as my agency grew).

If you are not keenly aware of and carefully watching the numbers at your agency, a bad month or two could spell disaster for your business. Of the many numbers you should be tracking, monthly and annual costs are among the most important.

If you have a handful of employees, you are likely using some accounting software to help manage your business. If this is not the case, I highly recommend you make that change immediately. (QuickBooks™ is the most common, and a great choice.) Hopefully, you have an accountant who has helped you organize your accounting software into logical categories for your transactions to help you understand your expenses. For the upcoming calculation examples, we'll use the following business expense categories. If you already use QuickBooks™ or another accounting software then extracting your expense numbers should be pretty simple. If you aren't currently using accounting software, here are some common expense categories to help you figure out your business expenses.

- **Payroll** (employee wages including your wages, Social Security and Medicare taxes as well as state and Federal Unemployment Tax for employees, payroll processing)
- **Occupancy** (office rent or purchase payment, common area maintenance "CAM" fees)
- **Utilities** (water, gas, electric, internet access)
- **Office Supplies** (everything from printer ink to paper clips)
- **Equipment** (computers, monitors, printers, and other equipment necessary to run your business)

*

If you are not keenly aware of and carefully watching the numbers at your agency, a bad month or two could spell disaster for your business.

- **Marketing and Advertising** (business networking, trade shows, social / traditional ads, website hosting, Pay Per Click advertising)
- **Health Insurance** (company portion of employee health insurance premiums)
- **Subscriptions and Software Licenses** (Adobe Creative Cloud, online education services, SaaS tools, and any other services with a monthly fee)
- **Food** (employee lunches, stocking the office refrigerator, and any other benefits you provide for employees)
- **Business Insurance** (errors and omissions insurance, liability insurance)

Are you unsure where your expenses should be categorized? Check with your accountant to come up with a strategy that meets the specific needs of your business.

Let's assume you have six employees, plus yourself, and that your monthly expenses are as follows:

Budget Category	Monthly Overhead Expenses	Annual Overhead Expenses
Payroll	$35,500	$426,000
Occupancy	$3,500	$42,000
Utilities	$1,000	$12,000
Office Supplies	$500	$6,000
Equipment	$1,000	$12,000
Marketing & Advertising	$1,500	$18,000
Health Insurance	$4,200	$50,400
Subscriptions & Software	$500	$6,000
Food	$500	$6,000
Business Insurance	$500	$6,000
TOTAL EXPENSES	$48,700	$584,400

Now that we know your monthly expenses, let's examine your team and their available billable hours. Billable hours are defined as the amount of time you can charge a client for an employee's work. In other words, it is the amount of time that an employee can work on paying projects. For example, your office manager is likely invaluable to your company, but most often, none of their tasks contribute directly to paying projects. Whereas, a programmer may spend most or all of their time doing tasks necessary to fulfill requests for paying customers. In this case, the percentage of the programmer's time that would be considered "billable" is 100%.

The question you need to ask yourself is, "How much of each employee's time is potentially used on tasks for paying projects?"

Unless you track hours over a span of time, you will just have to make your best guess for these numbers. For example, if you, as the owner of the agency, spend a large amount of your time doing sales and accounting, you may only have 40% of your time available to do client work. However, your programmer, Peter, doesn't spend much time doing anything but coding, therefore, 80% of his time can potentially be used for client paid work. Our objective is to determine the total number of potentially billable hours across all of the employees in your business.

By the way, I think it is reasonable to assume that the maximum someone would be able to spend doing work for paying clients is 80% of their business day. Look around your office, nobody is 100% billable when you add in meetings, water cooler time, breaks, vacations, and foosball. When you do this exercise for your business, I recommend that you use 80% as your maximum.

To calculate the number of production hours available for each employee, we will simply use the same method I presented in the previous section. Start with 2,080 total hours for a full-time employee (40 hours per week multiplied by 52 weeks in a year) and multiply it by the percentage of potentially billable hours for each person to calculate their total number of potential production hours.

I've included the chart again here based on 5% increments. The first column shows 2,080 potentially billable hours per year. The second column is the percentage of time available to be used on paying client work. The final column shows the total number of annual production hours adjusted by the corresponding percentage.

Annual Production Hours	Billable Percentage	Adjusted Annual Production Hours
2,080	100%	2,080
2,080	95%	1,976
2,080	90%	1,872
2,080	85%	1,768
2,080	80%	1,664
2,080	75%	1,560
2,080	70%	1,456
2,080	65%	1,352
2,080	60%	1,248
2,080	55%	1,144
2,080	50%	1,040
2,080	45%	936
2,080	40%	832
2,080	35%	728
2,080	30%	624
2,080	25%	520
2,080	20%	416
2,080	15%	312
2,080	10%	208
2,080	5%	104
2,080	0%	0

Analyzing how many billable hours each team member has to offer is a critical step, enabling you to calculate an accurate hourly burn rate. Let's examine a hypothetical list of an agency with seven employees. The table below shows each employee, the percentage of time they have available for client work (billable percentage), and the number of annual production hours.

Employee	Billable Percentage	Annual Production Hours
You (President & ECD)	40%	832
Sally (Art Director)	60%	1,248
John (Designer)	80%	1,664
Olga (Designer)	80%	1,664
Peter (Programmer)	80%	1,664
Anton (Account Manager)	15%	312
Sasha (Office Manager)	0%	0
TOTAL ANNUAL PRODUCTION HOURS		7,384

Based on this calculation, the agency has 7,384 production hours each year to cover the annual expenses of $584,400 (see pg. 28).

Sasha, the office manager, doesn't do any tasks that are billable to a client and doesn't contribute any production hours to the total. Sally, the art director, spends time in sales meetings with you, therefore, she only has 60% of her time available for client paid work. John, Olga, and Peter are the most "heads down" employees and the majority of their available time (80%) can be spent working on projects for paying clients.

Now, let's calculate the hourly burn rate for your agency by dividing the total annual expenses by the total annual production hours.

	Annual Expenses
÷	**Annual Production Hours**
	Hourly Burn Rate

In this case our calculation would be…

	$584,400	Annual Expenses
÷	**7,384**	Annual Production Hours
	$79.14	Hourly Burn Rate

As a reminder, you should always round up, even if "math rules" say otherwise. This makes your hourly burn rate: $80. We always round up because it is better to err on the side of more profit, rather than less. In this situation, when you are considering pricing your work based on your cost, you must charge a minimum of $80 per hour to break even on a project.

$80	Hourly Burn Rate (Rounded Up)

Keep in mind that this method is used to calculate a blended hourly burn rate across all of your employees. The reality is your art director's time probably costs more than your designer's time, and you could get really crazy by attempting to calculate your project by project cost based on the estimated time spent by each unique employee. However, a blended hourly burn rate is usually sufficient when pricing your agency's work.

Ok. I realize that this may seem a bit complicated at first. But like I have stated before, once you dig in it really isn't too tough and it is imperative that you know this number so you can price your projects profitably. Please take the time to calculate your hourly burn rate using the following worksheet to help you determine your number.

*

Always round up, even if "math rules" say you should round down. It is better to err on the side of more profit, rather than less.

Hourly Burn Rate Scenario 03 Worksheet

Calculating Your Hourly Burn Rate Based on Agency Overhead Expenses

Step 01:

Enter the monthly expenses for your agency and then add up the total. Your goal is to discover all the costs you have to run your business. (If you use QuickBooks™ or another accounting software, you will likely be able to skip this step by exporting the information from your software.)

Budget Category	Monthly Overhead Expenses
Payroll	
Occupancy	
Utilities	
Office Supplies	
Equipment	
Marketing & Advertising	
Health Insurance	
Subscriptions & Software	
Food	
Business Insurance	
Other	
TOTAL MONTHLY EXPENSES	$

Step 02:

Take your total monthly expenses from Step 01 and multiply by twelve (for twelve months in a year). This calculation will unveil your total annual expenses.

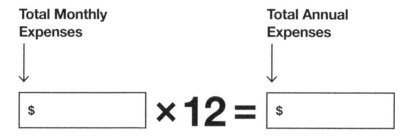

Total Monthly Expenses		**Total Annual Expenses**
↓		↓
$	**×12=**	$

By the way, we won't be calculating estimated taxes for an agency (like we did in Scenario 02) because the tax implication is distributed among the employees in the "payroll" budget category. In the United States, most agencies are set up as a Limited Liability Company (LLC) or an S-Corporation. In each of these business structures, the owner(s) of the company will owe taxes on any profit not distributed to themselves or their employees through payroll.

Step 03:

List all of your employees, including yourself, and estimate their percentage of available billable time. For example, if your office manager doesn't produce any billable work for your customers, you would enter 0%. If you have a programmer who does nothing but code you would enter 80%. (Remember, a maximum of 80% for any employee.) After you determine the billable percentage for each employee, use the chart on the following page and list their adjusted annual production hours. Then total up the column to calculate the total annual production hours for your agency.

Employee	Billable Percentage	Adjusted Annual Production Hours
TOTAL ANNUAL PRODUCTION HOURS		

Annual Production Hours	Billable Percentage	Adjusted Annual Production Hours
2,080	100%	2,080
2,080	95%	1,976
2,080	90%	1,872
2,080	85%	1,768
2,080	80%	1,664
2,080	75%	1,560
2,080	70%	1,456
2,080	65%	1,352
2,080	60%	1,248
2,080	55%	1,144
2,080	50%	1,040
2,080	45%	936
2,080	40%	832
2,080	35%	728
2,080	30%	624
2,080	25%	520
2,080	20%	416
2,080	15%	312
2,080	10%	208
2,080	5%	104
2,080	0%	0

Step 04:

Calculate the hourly burn rate for your agency by dividing your total annual expenses from Step 02 by your total annual production hours from Step 03.

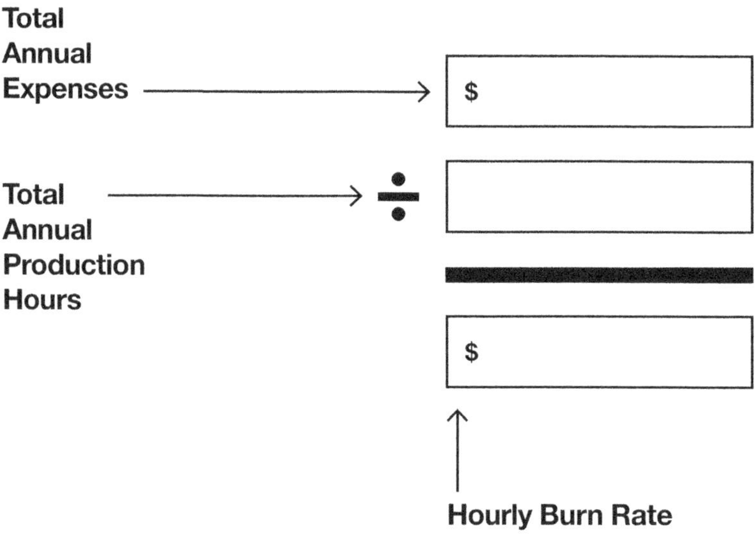

*

You cannot profitably price projects without understanding the costs of your business and calculating your hourly burn rate.

Calculating Estimated Production Hours for a Project

I have used many different methods to estimate the number of hours it will take to complete a project. Some of them are fairly time consuming, like interviewing my team members who will be working on the project to itemizing all the necessary info on complicated spreadsheets. Others are simple and quick, like using the exact number of hours we logged on the last project that matches the scope of the current project we are trying to estimate.

For the sake of the content in this book, I will share with you one of the methods that is both effective and pretty accurate, without being overly laborious.

The method I will share should help you break down a project into segments based on the number of delivery rounds you will include in the project scope. The unofficial industry standard number of delivery and feedback rounds for a graphic design project is three. I always love it when the client approves things in round two, and we all cringe when things get out of control with five or six rounds (or worse). Once, I went more than 30 rounds on a logo design with a client early in my career. (I probably should have sent them a change order. Live and learn.)

That said, the average number of rounds is three and many projects can be completed within those rounds, assuming your client is able to navigate the feedback from their team without much difficulty.

The unofficial industry standard number of delivery and feedback rounds for graphic design projects is three.

Three rounds of feedback usually flows like this:

Delivery Rounds	Delivered By	Description
Round 1	Agency	The agency sends the first set of design comps to the client.
Feedback	Client	The client provides feedback on the designs from Round 1.
Round 2	Agency	The agency makes changes and sends revised designs to the client.
Feedback	Client	The client provides feedback on the designs from Round 2.
Round 3	Agency	The agency makes changes and sends the revised designs to the client.
Feedback	Client	The client provides feedback on the designs from Round 3.
Final Delivery	Agency	The agency makes the requested changes for the designs and packages up the final files for delivery.

One could argue that there are actually four rounds of designs delivered to the client, which I suppose is true. However, when planning delivery "rounds," this project flow provides the client with three opportunities to provide feedback (which is what they will be most interested in).

I have tried unsuccessfully to cut this project flow down a few times over my career. Through these attempts, I have found it is extremely difficult to get projects consistently approved with less opportunities for client feedback than three.

You should define each delivery round in your project contract and hold yourself and your client to those rounds. Any additional rounds should cost the client more money. Extra rounds should always be discussed with your client and clearly understood before doing the work and before sending an invoice.

I had an outsourced agency send me an invoice for $20,000 for extra rounds of changes which they had never discussed with me in advance. Ouch! They hadn't kept me abreast of how the project was

*

Breaking down a project into rounds during the estimating process will help you get a more accurate appraisal of the number of hours it will require to produce the work.

tracking against the approved budget. Once the project was completed, we never used that agency again. I highly recommend you discuss matters of money with your clients prior to sending the bill.

Ok, back to the feedback rounds discussion. The three round project flow that I presented early could be written in simpler terms as follows.

Delivery Rounds
R1 Delivery
R1 Feedback
R2 Delivery
R2 Feedback
R3 Delivery
R3 Feedback
Final Delivery

Breaking the project down into these rounds will help us get a more accurate estimation of the number of hours it will take to produce the work. I'll explain how this is done by presenting an example.

A client approaches you to design a logo for their company. You discuss the project with them and have a pretty clear understanding of their vision for the logo. You decide that you will deliver five different logo designs for review in Round 1. You anticipate a day to produce the five different logo designs (8 hours). The client will provide you feedback on Round 1 and you estimate that Round 2 will take you roughly one half of a day to produce new logo design options (4 hours). Next, the client will give feedback on the Round 2 designs and you will modify the logos and delivery Round 3. You estimate that this phase will take you another half of a day (4 hours). Finally, the client provides you with feedback on Round 3 and you will make the final changes, export a final package of logos in various file types, and deliver them to your client. You expect an additional half of a day of work to produce the delivery files (4 hours).

A more structured way of detailing the project flow could be outlined in a table format. Your project contract should include a description of the rounds included in the project scope. However, I would dissuade you from including the estimated time needed to complete each round in your proposal. **You only estimate time for each round to help you know your break-even price on the project; don't share your hours with the client.** This calculation influences your pricing in that it guarantees profitability. This will become more clear in the coming chapters. So, stay tuned.

Delivery Rounds	Description	Estimated Time
R1 Delivery	The agency will deliver five initial logo designs for client review.	8 hours
R1 Feedback	The client will provide feedback on the initial designs sent in Round 1.	0.5 hours
R2 Delivery	The agency will make the changes requested by the client and deliver new logo design options.	4 hours
R2 Feedback	The client will provide feedback on the designs sent in Round 2.	0.5 hours
R3 Delivery	The agency will make the client changes and deliver new logo design options.	4 hours
R3 Feedback	The client will provide feedback on the initial designs sent in Round 3.	0.5 hours
Final Delivery	The agency will make the final changes requested by the client and package final designs for delivery.	4 hours
TOTAL ESTIMATED PRODUCTION HOURS		21.5

Breaking down a project into rounds and then estimating the number of hours it will take you to do the work for each round helps you avoid underestimating a project. This method allows us to examine the project hours more closely than just guessing on the project as a whole. It also yields a much more accurate estimation of the real level of effort needed to produce the work.

Calculating Production Cost

Now that all of the complicated calculations are solved, let's talk about how to estimate your production cost for a project. This is a simple calculation made by multiplying the number of production hours that you estimate it will take to complete the work by your hourly burn rate, and then adding in any hard costs you will have for the project.

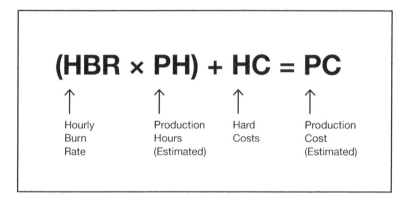

$$(HBR \times PH) + HC = PC$$

↑	↑	↑	↑
Hourly Burn Rate	Production Hours (Estimated)	Hard Costs	Production Cost (Estimated)

Hard Costs

Beyond the time necessary to produce the work, there may be additional hard costs that you should consider when pricing a project. The hard costs could include things like renting camera equipment for a photo shoot, purchasing specific stock photography, outsourcing to other designers or programmers who may have provided you with a fixed bid price for their services, purchasing specific software needed to complete the work, and many other types of costs beyond your time. Hard costs should always be accounted for when you are pricing your projects.

Let's use this formula in combination with the three scenarios we examined earlier. This should help you understand the process more clearly as you prepare to calculate your production cost for future projects.

Example 01: Part-time Freelancer

Let's say you are a part-time freelancer and your client is asking you to design a logo. You have determined that your time is worth \$60,000 per year (an hourly burn rate of \$28.85, which we will round up to \$29). You broke out the rounds and estimate that it will take you 21.5 hours to design the logo (including three rounds of client feedback). Now multiply 21.5 hours by your hourly burn rate of \$29 to yield \$623.50 before adding in any hard costs. This only represents the cost of your production hours.

On this project, you don't anticipate having any additional hard costs to include in your price. Your hard cost price is \$0, so your total estimated production cost is \$623.50.

If you charge your client less than \$623.50, you are doing the work at an unprofitable rate. Anything you charge beyond \$623.50 is extra profit in your pocket. If you finish the project in less than 21.5 hours, you make extra profit. If it takes you more than 21.5 hours, you are losing money.

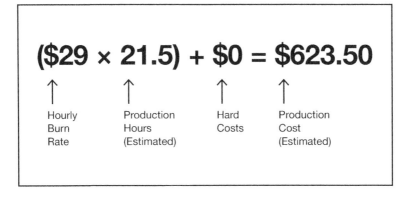

$$(\$29 \times 21.5) + \$0 = \$623.50$$

\$29	21.5	\$0	\$623.50
↑ Hourly Burn Rate	↑ Production Hours (Estimated)	↑ Hard Costs	↑ Production Cost (Estimated)

Example 02: Full-time Freelancer

Here is an example assuming you are a full-time freelancer and you have calculated your hourly burn rate to be $50. You are responding to a client's request to design a tri-fold brochure. Approximately 35 hours are needed to complete the work. Simply multiply your burn rate of $50 per hour by 35 hours and you find that the cost of your production hours is $1,750 before adding hard costs.

You have hired an external freelancer to help produce some of the initial comps. She is charging you a fixed price of $300 for the work she is producing. This is a hard cost on the project.

Now, add your production hours cost of $1,750 to your hard costs of $300 and you will find your estimated production cost for the project is $2,050.

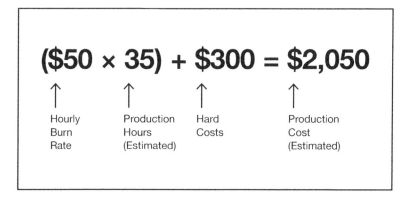

$$(\$50 \times 35) + \$300 = \$2{,}050$$

$50 ↑	35 ↑	$300 ↑	$2,050 ↑
Hourly Burn Rate	Production Hours (Estimated)	Hard Costs	Production Cost (Estimated)

Example 03: Small Agency

Finally, let's look at an example of a small agency with four employees. You have calculated your hourly burn rate to be $60. Your client requests your services to design new packaging for one of their products. Based on the project scope, you expect the project to require 70 hours spread across your talented team. Calculate your production hours cost by multiplying your $60 hourly burn rate by the 70 hours you estimate needing to complete the work. This yields $4,200 before adding in hard costs.

One of your employees is a talented photographer, but you need to rent some equipment to produce the photography included in the project scope. The equipment rental will be a hard cost of $450. In addition to the equipment rental, you are hiring an external illustrator to create some icons for the packaging. The illustrator has given you a price of $350 for their work. Between the camera equipment rental and the outsourced illustration, your hard costs total $800.

Now add the cost of your production hours ($4,200) to your hard costs to calculate your estimated production cost: $6,000.

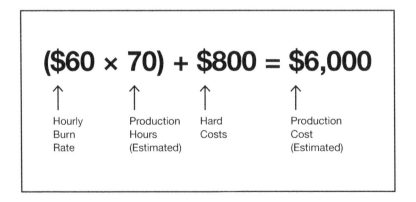

$$(\$60 \times 70) + \$800 = \$6{,}000$$

($60	× 70)	+ $800	= $6,000
↑ Hourly Burn Rate	↑ Production Hours (Estimated)	↑ Hard Costs	↑ Production Cost (Estimated)

*

Production cost is calculated by multiplying the hourly burn rate by the estimated production hours and adding hard costs.

Variable 01: Production Cost Worksheet

Estimating Production Cost for a Project

Step 01:

List all the delivery and feedback rounds you intend to include in the scope of the project. Add a brief description of what will happen in each round (how many design comps you will include, etc.). Estimate the amount of time you anticipate spending to complete each round. Be sure to include time for client feedback rounds, as you will likely spend time on a phone call, in a meeting, or, at minimum, reviewing the client's written feedback. Finally, total the number of estimated production hours at the bottom of the table.

Delivery Rounds	Description	Estimated Time
TOTAL ESTIMATED PRODUCTION HOURS		

Step 02:

Calculate your hourly burn rate using one of the worksheets provided in this book (pgs. 12, 19, or 35). Multiply your hourly burn rate by the estimated production hours from Step 01. This calculation will yield the cost of your time to produce the work (in other words, your production hours cost).

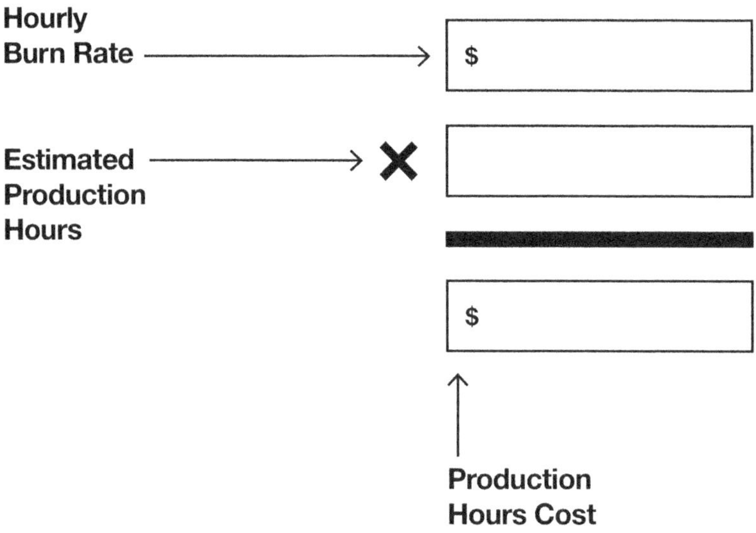

Step 03:

List all of the hard costs you anticipate for this project. Hard costs are any costs you will have above and beyond your time to produce the work. These costs include things like stock photography licenses, outsourced pricing to a freelancer or agency (if you are having someone help produce the work), custom photo shoots, equipment rentals or purchases required to complete the project, printing costs, and any other items you will need to spend money on to complete the work. Enter a brief description of the hard cost and corresponding prices.

Hard Cost Item	Description	Price
TOTAL HARD COSTS		

Step 04:

Add your production hours cost calculated in Step 02 to the hard costs that you defined in Step 03. This calculation will yield your total estimated production cost.

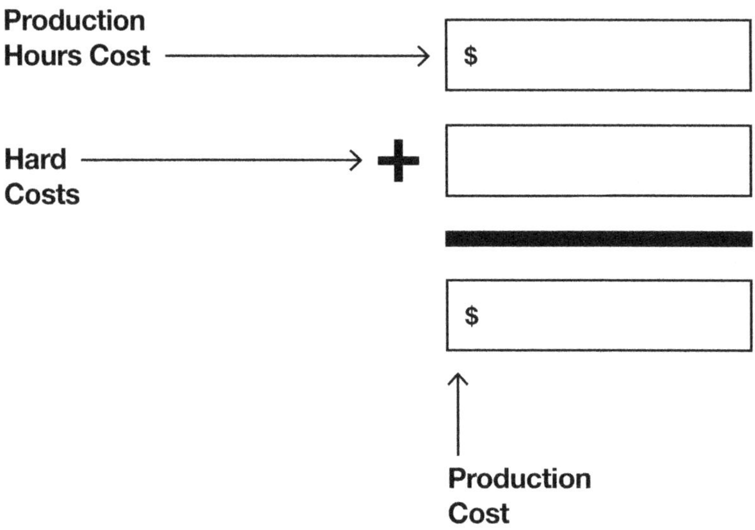

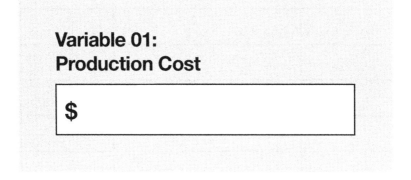

Variable 01: Production Cost

$

Congratulations! You now have the necessary tools for calculating your cost to produce a project. The estimated production cost variable is critically important, as it can either make or break your profitability on a project. We will use this variable when deciding on a project price using a pricing spectrum which I will explain soon. Stay with me!

*

The production cost variable is critically important, as it can either make or break your profitability on a project.

04

CHAPTER 04

Variable 02: Market Value

The market value of a product or service is equal to the amount that someone is willing to pay for it. No more. No less.

The challenge with pricing graphic design work based on market value is that the perception of value varies wildly from client to client. A $2,000 logo to one customer may be perceived as the deal of the century, but to another client, the price may seem extremely high. These two clients have very different perceptions of the value of the logo. Which client is right?

A $2,000 logo to one customer may be perceived as the deal of the century, but to another client, the price may seem extremely high.

This concept holds true across all industries. If I think my home is worth $800,000, but I can only find a buyer willing to pay $650,000, then I have an inaccurate perception of the market value of my home. People regularly spend $40 or $50 on the cheapest T-shirt that can be manufactured because they can only get it at a concert. Take the concert logos and imagery off, and that same T-shirt might only have a market value of $5 (and the retailer would still make a profit). The

*

The market value of a product or service is equal to the amount that someone is willing to pay for it. No more. No less.

point is that the market value of the T-shirt isn't based solely on the manufacturing cost. This concept holds true in the creative industry; we cannot charge our clients based on the production cost variable alone. We must look at the market value of the work we produce.

You may be asking yourself, "So how do I know the market value of my work?" I'm glad you asked.

Market Value Based on Return on Investment (ROI)

The first way market value can be considered is based upon the return on investment (ROI) that your client receives from your work. Let's say you create a marketing campaign that increases your client's annual revenue from $1,000,000 to $3,000,000. A $2,000,000 return on investment is considerable. Now, if you charged the client $10,000 for the campaign, that is a GREAT investment for the client. If the client spent $2,500,000 on the campaign, then the return on investment is negative and the campaign was a failure.

The challenge with pricing work based on the value of the return on investment is that it is almost impossible to know how much revenue your work will produce for your client before it produces the revenue. Will the $10,000 of work you produce for your customer yield them $20,000 of profit? How can you know in advance?

If you are committed to charging your client based on the return on investment value of your work, there are two ways you can potentially sell a client your design services.

First, you must have a proven track record of success. If you can say to a client, "Here is work we did for client XYZ. It yielded a huge return on investment for the client. They spent $20,000 with our agency. Our work increased sales by $100,000 and generated $60,000 in profit for their business. We can do a similar project for you and would expect you to yield a similar return on your investment."

The second way to sell a client based on ROI is through a "pay for performance" agreement. In this model, you really put your money where your mouth is. I know a great agency that built their business on this model. Simply put, they only charge their clients for the sales they close. The agency pays for all of the strategy, design, development, call centers, websites, and other marketing materials necessary to close deals. When the agency sells a customer for their client, the client pays them a contracted fee for the acquisition of the customer. This has been a great business model for both the agency and the client.

A few of the challenges that dissuade most designers from engaging in business structures like this are first, most agencies don't have the financial resources to pay up front for the project with the hope of revenue at some point in the future. Most agencies and designers are not willing to take that risk.

Second, agencies (and especially freelancers) cannot wait extended time periods to receive payment for the return on the investment. These types of arrangements often have long payment cycles.

Third, it is extremely complicated, in most circumstances, to track the return. Debates between the client and the agency as to which marketing efforts actually contributed to closing the sale of the customer often ensue. As a result, this type of payment structure is not recommended for most designers, nor would it be their preference, so we won't delve more deeply into it here.

Market Value Based on Competition

The method we will use to calculate the market value variable is to consider what our competitors charge for the same type of work. This will help us determine what pricing the market will bear for our services. There are several methods to help you determine the market value of the work you are doing for your customers.

Survey Your Clients

Don't be afraid to ask your clients what they have spent on design services in the past. When you get the data, start tracking it somewhere. Many clients are happy to share this information and if you ask it in the right way, it isn't awkward.

*

Don’t be afraid to ask your clients what they have spent on design services in the past. More often than not, people are happy to share numbers.

"Hey, Joe, if you don't mind me asking, how much did you spend on the last few websites you had created? I am always looking to stay competitive in my pricing."

"Hey, Sally, do you mind if I ask you a few questions? I am trying to make sure I am staying competitive in my pricing. If you were going to outsource a logo design, how much would you expect to budget for it? How about a tri-fold brochure? What about a billboard design?"

These types of questions work great if you have a strong relationship with your client. I have found that more often than not, people are happy to share numbers. Surveying your clients works especially well when you don't have an active project with them. It is easy to ask in an informal manner, over lunch or on the phone. Give it a try and be sure to track the responses to begin building an understanding of the perceived market value of the services you offer.

Review Industry Surveys

Every few years the Graphic Artist Guild publishes a new edition of the *Graphic Artists Guild Handbook: Pricing & Ethical Guidelines*. This is an incredible resource for both pricing surveys, as well as contract language and other valuable insights. Every independent designer should own a copy. The book contains a compilation of average prices for everything from packaging design to illustration. Many of the prices are organized by client size or circulation volume of the final artwork.

Now, a word of caution. When I first started using this book about three years into my agency's lifespan, I remember thinking, "Man, if I was charging these kinds of prices, I would be making a lot more money!" The fact is that my little six person agency based in a mid-sized market could not command the price ranges I was seeing in these industry surveys. However, within a few short years, as we grew our agency and reputation, we were able to charge the higher-end prices in many of the categories. So, if you are like the young me thinking that the survey prices are crazy high, just keep working to develop your skill set and give yourself time.

Finally, you can review various industry surveys online. A simple internet search for "average price of a website" or "average price of brochure design" yields plenty of blog posts, message board threads, and articles to help you get a sense of the market value of your work based on the thoughts and comments from other people in the industry.

Leverage Your Experience

The final way to understand market value by getting a sense of what competitors charge is to pay attention to the flow of business and leverage your experience.

Pay attention to what your clients say. Over the years I have gained a lot of insights from my clients letting something slip that they shouldn't have (like a competitor's price).

Pay attention to email threads. I have been the proud, accidental recipient of a lot of competitor proposals over the years when a client inadvertently forwards an emailed proposal to me. These are golden opportunities to discover how competitors propose and price their projects.

Pay attention to your win-loss record. What prices have been approved by your clients? What prices were too high? Be sure you are keeping a record of each proposal you deliver to a client, the price, and whether you won or lost the project. This is valuable information to analyze as you determine the market value of your work.

All of these items contribute to experience. As you continue to work as a designer, your market value intuition will grow exponentially from paying attention to your business dealings.

*

Over time you will develop a keen sense of what the market will bear for different types of products and services. Each client is different. Each city is different.

Establishing Market Value

Over time you will develop a keen sense of what the market will bear for different types of products and services. Each client is different. Each city is different.

The market value of the work we did for businesses based in Los Angeles and New York City differed from businesses based in Salt Lake City and other smaller markets. The work may have taken the same amount of time to create, but the market value was different based on the client's geographic location and industry.

Developing market value intuition by surveying your clients, reviewing industry surveys, and paying attention to the ebb and flow of your business takes some time. In preparation for this variable in our pricing spectrum, let's look at a few examples of how this is done during the estimation process.

Example 01: Logo Design for a Local Client

Let's say a local client approaches you with a request to design a new logo for their business.

Survey Your Clients: Right out of the gate you think to yourself, "I just asked a similar client what they have spent on logo design projects in the past and they told me around $1,500."

Review Industry Surveys: Next, you open up the *Graphic Artist Guild Handbook* and discover that based on industry standards for clients of this size, a logo design project should range from $1,800 to $5,000.

Leverage Your Experience: Finally, you know, based on past experience, that similar types of clients have approved logo design prices as high as $2,000. You are also aware that you lost the last three logo design bids you sent for $2,500. From this experience you get a sense of the pricing threshold.

Now that you have done your research and considerations, it is time to pick a market value price for the project. In this situation, my personal inner dialogue would be as follows, "Ok, $1,500 is a solid starting place, but the *Graphic Artist Guild Handbook* says that it is probably a little low. I also know I have been green lighting logos around $2,000 over the past six months, but I lost a couple bids at $2,500. So, the low-end price from the *Graphic Artist Guild Handbook* of $1,800 is probably about the market value threshold of this project. I'll go with that for my market value variable."

Example 02: Website Design by a Small Agency

The bigger the project, the wider variance in the perceived market value. Let's examine a scenario where a client requests a ten page informational website for their business and you run a small agency with five employees.

Survey Your Clients: You recently asked one of your clients what they think the design and development of a corporate brochure website would cost and they told you they have paid $15,000 to $20,000 for those types of projects in the past.

Review Industry Surveys: You consulted the *Graphic Artist Guild Handbook* and found the prices for these types of websites based on your region range from $30,000 to $50,000.

Leverage Your Experience: You recently heard one of your competitors was charging a minimum of $25,000 for websites and you know you do better work.

With an understanding of these numbers, your inner dialogue might going something like this, "Alright, $15,000 is the low-end for this type of work, but that is half of minimum amount the *Graphic Artist Handbook* says we should be charging. The handbook also says that these can be as high as $50,000. My competitor is charging at least $25,000 for this type of work. Hmmm...looks like the market value is probably somewhere between $25,000 and $35,000. I think I'll go with $30,000 as my number for the market value variable."

The market value variable will have a big impact on your pricing considerations. Take the time to survey your clients, review industry standards, and leverage your experience to determine the market value for your projects.

Variable 02: Market Value Worksheet

Establishing the Market Value of a Project

Step 01: Survey Your Clients

How much have your clients spent on similar projects in the past? Don't be afraid to ask the client who is requesting this project, as well as any other clients you may feel comfortable asking. Try to survey at least three different sources. It is best to try to survey companies matching your current client's size and type of business. Enter your survey results in the table below by listing the type of project (tri-fold brochure, logo design, full page magazine ad, or whatever the project may be). Then list the source (client or company name) of the information. Finally, include the price.

Project Type	Client Name	Price

Step 02: Industry Surveys

Review design industry surveys in an effort to determine what other agencies are charging for the type of work you are bidding. The *Graphic Artists Guild Handbook: Pricing & Ethical Guidelines* is always a great first resource to review. You can also search online in an effort to find other surveys, blog articles, and message board posts that divulge industry pricing. For example, if you are bidding a logo, try a search for "How much should a logo design cost?" (My recent Google search on this question revealed 1.4 billion results.)

Project Type	Source	Price

Step 03: Leverage Your Experience

What projects have you done in the past that are similar to this project? What price did you propose to your client? Did they green light the project? Use the tables below to list similar projects you have won in the past, along with projects lost and their corresponding prices.

Projects Won

Project Type	Client Name	Price

Projects Lost

Project Type	Client Name	Price

Step 04: Establish a Market Value

Finally, take some time to consider the data you have gathered and establish a market value price for the project. We will use this number in our pricing spectrum process.

If you are just getting started in your design career and do not have any clients to survey or much experience to leverage, you can probably get info using the industry surveys. The objective of this worksheet is to help you gather enough data to determine a market value price as closely as possible.

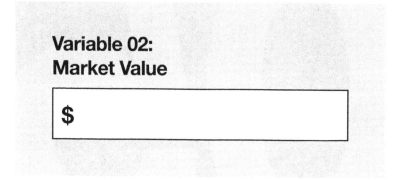

Variable 02: Market Value

$

05

CHAPTER 05

Variable 03: Client Budget

The final variable we need to analyze when pricing our work is the client's budget. How much are they willing to spend on the work they are requesting?

Budgets for design work vary greatly from client to client and region to region. I recently consulted with a client whose CEO was convinced that design work was a commodity only meriting the efforts of interns. As a result, the client's budgets for design were very low. On the contrary, a client who values design will likely have higher budgets appropriate for their projects. The value a client places upon design work is proportional with the budget they allocate.

The budget number is an extremely critical variable to know before choosing your price. It is rare that a client will increase their budget to work with you. Nine times out of ten, if their budget is set, it is set. Unchangeable.

Nine times out of ten, if the client's budget is set, it is set. Unchangeable.

Of course, there are tactics you can use in your salesmanship to encourage the client to increase their budget, and we will discuss some of those techniques at the end of this chapter. However, in my experience, when someone successfully sells the client on increasing their budget, there is a great risk with the client becoming combative

*

All the sales tactics in the world will not be able to sell the client on increasing their budget for a logo design from $3,000 to $8,000 if they are only in possession of $3,000.

and increasing pressure on the designer to perform at an unreasonable level. The client expects a bigger return on their bigger investment.

Ultimately, all the sales tactics in the world will not be able to sell the client on increasing their budget for a logo design from $3,000 to $8,000 if they are only in possession of $3,000. That is the money they have to spend and with networks such as Fiverr and Upwork/Elance at their fingertips, your client can always find someone cheaper to do the work. Our objective in analyzing the client's budget is to determine whether or not it makes sense for <u>you</u> to do the work within their budget or not.

How to Extract a Client's Budget

In my book, *Burn Your Portfolio*, I present several strategies for "How to Flush Out a Budget." We'll review those here and consider a few more to help you determine a number for the budget based pricing variable.

Ask the Client

The most direct approach to determining your client's budget is to ask them. Far too many designers are afraid to even ask the question. Get over it. Time is money. No sense in messing around scoping a project if you don't even know whether your client has an appropriate amount of budget allocated to complete the work.

To ensure that you don't come across as a gold digger, I recommend you discuss the project with the client first. Ask a lot of questions. Take notes. Make sure that you have a clear understanding of the scope of work. Then, at the end of the conversation, ask with confidence the following question:

"Alright, Anna, this is all great information. I think that gives me a pretty clear picture of what you are wanting to accomplish. Is there a budget range you are shooting to work within?"

The client usually responds in one of two ways.

The first common response is, "We don't really know yet. We are getting several bids and then deciding our budget."

This type of client is going to make you work a bit harder to find out their number and you'll have to resort to one of the other tactics. Don't just fly past the question. They have a number in their head. It may not be an exact budget number, but they have a number they're hoping for or at least a price threshold with which they are comfortable. Take the time to figure it out.

The second common response is, "We are trying to be below $X,XXX." This response is probably much more common than you think. Organized clients who understand the value of the work you produce will often share their budget number with you.

Another type of client that will frequently share their budget number is the cheapskate client. You know who they are. The ones who are looking for a deal and they know the only chance they have of getting you to do the work is by dangling their insufficient budget in your face, hoping you're desperate enough to take it. This type of client is preying upon your hunger for work or your need to please with "the client is always right" mentality. Maybe you'll be willing to give them a deal, maybe not. We'll analyze that psychology later.

Cheapskate clients with insufficient budgets always seem to come with promises of future glory. I have been promised trillions of dollars "tomorrow" to help with a project that had no budget "today." (The client literally said "trillions." True story.) One client offered to give our agency a freezer full of buffalo steaks as partial payment (which we never received). These unfunded clients always try to convince you that "you are going to want to be a part of this" or that "they know a lot of people," as if those things will somehow yield future income for your agency. As for me, I trade creative services for money. That is it, plain and simple. If the client has no money now, it is extremely likely they will have no money later.

Poker Face

No matter what the client tells you, when they share their budget, it is best to muster your most capable poker face. Try not to give them a sense of whether you think their budget is too big or too small. You can address budget with them later if it isn't sufficient for you to take on the project. For now, your only objective is to get a number for the budget variable. You'll analyze the pricing after the meeting.

It is best to muster your most capable poker face. Try not to give them a sense of whether you think their budget is too big or too small.

"Budget poker face" is as important with big budgets as it is with small budgets. The economic recession from 2008 hit my agency pretty hard and I hemorrhaged money keeping my agency afloat. We were finally getting back on track in early 2010 when an internationally recognized beverage company approached us to create an innovative website for one of their brands. In their request for proposal, they outlined the project goals, scope, timeline, and shared their budget of $120,000. After grinding out a meager profit in 2009, that project budget represented the ability to get my agency back on track for 2010. Inside, I was shouting for joy.

But sharing that joy and relief would have alarmed the client to our unstable financial situation and likely rattled their confidence in our ability to do the job. Although we had completed many projects with similar scope before the recession, they didn't know we hadn't greenlit a project like that in almost two years. We bid the work based on their budget and they confidently selected our agency. We did an amazing job on the project and it did, indeed, catapult us out of the economic recession and into an era of significant growth.

Ask About Past Projects

If your client is unwilling to give up their number when you ask for it, you'll have to resort to using another method. Asking them about their past projects can be a successful strategy.

"What have you spent on projects like this in the past?"

This question is similarly used in our effort to establish market value for the work and if you have asked them about past projects already, be sure not to use this tactic again to extract their budget.

Obviously, you should not use this approach if you already know they haven't had experience with projects like this. However, if you know they have worked with designers in the past to do similar work, don't be afraid to ask the question.

Float a Price Range

I use this approach all the time to successfully begin money conversations with clients. Simply float a price range of the past few projects you have done comparable to their project (or a price range you consider appropriate for the project, regardless of your past experience).

After you float out your price, pause for a moment and gauge the client's facial reaction and body language. If you see them squirm, you know that your proposed budget exceeds their comfort level.

"Similar projects we have done in the past have been between $4,000 and $6,000." *PAUSE.* "Does that fit within your budget expectations?"

If they are comfortable with your proposed price range, they will usually respond quickly with something like, "Yes, that seems in line with what we would expect."

*

If you see them squirm, you know that your proposed budget exceeds their comfort level.

Compare other Products

If your client is still being cryptic about their budget, you can always try comparing a different product or industry in an effort to at least gauge whether they are on the high-end or the low-end of the market value.

In this approach, I often use "cars" as the metaphor.

Start with something like, "I understand you aren't sure exactly what you want to spend on this project yet. Just to ensure we are targeting a budget that's in the ballpark of what you are hoping for, let's compare your project to cars."

You continue, "A Chevy Malibu and an Aston Martin Vantage will both get you from point A to point B; they both have four wheels and an engine, but they are very different types of transportation. The Aston Martin will include all kinds of high-end features and bells and whistles you won't find in the Chevy Malibu. Are you wanting something really high-end? Or are you just looking to get started and then plan to add higher-end features later?"

Most people get this metaphor and it can successfully help you understand the client's budget more clearly. People frequently enjoy having this conversation and oftentimes start trying to determine which car their budget corresponds with best.

This method works especially well if you are bidding on a digital product like a website or app where there is usually a dramatic difference between a low-end product and a high-end product.

Send a Rough Estimate

If you ever have concerns that the client does not have sufficient budget for the work and you have struggled to get them to discuss budget numbers, consider sending them a very brief, one page estimate. When I use this approach, I create a one page PDF that contains a summary of the project and a budget. I deliver this to the client including a description email similar to the following:

"Hi, Joan! Thank you for considering us for your project. We think our agency would be a great fit to successfully complete the work for your company. Before we take the time to detail out the entire project scope, we thought it would be best to send you a quick estimate to make sure we are on the same page. Please see the attached PDF document containing a summary of the project, as we understand it, along with an estimated price range.

"If this seems in harmony with your expectations, our next step would be to provide you with a full proposal that details each aspect of the project along with a committed price from our agency to complete the job.

"Please reach out if you have any questions. I look forward to hearing from you!"

This method can save you many hours of crafting proposals for clients who are insincere or unrealistic in their budget expectations. Based upon their response, you will either proceed to create a full proposal or gracefully withdraw from the bidding process.

The budget variable is the final critical component for determining your price. It is so critical, in fact, that if you cannot extract a number from your client even with the previously mentioned tactics, you'll have to guess the budget variable when you create your pricing spectrum. If you don't know the client's budget, you will be firing blind, possibly missing the target completely.

Example Budget Extraction Conversation

Let's examine how a budget conversation might happen with a client who is reluctant to share their numbers with you.

The Scene: *You and your client are wrapping up the discovery meeting for their project. You have asked a lot of questions and taken robust notes. The client has not divulged their budget.*

Agency: "Thank you for this information. I think we have a pretty thorough understanding of the project scope. Is there a budget range you are trying to work within?"

Client: "Well, we aren't exactly sure. Right now we are just getting bids from a few agencies."

Agency: "I see. Before we spend time crafting a proposal, it would be great to know if we are targeting the right price range, or if we should look at ways to modify the scope to get the price to fit within your comfort level. What have you spent on projects like this in the past?"

Client: "We haven't really done any projects like this previously. So we aren't quite sure."

Agency: "That's fine. We will probably be a great fit for you, because we have done a lot of projects like this. The past few projects we have completed similar to this one came in around $4,000 to $6,000. Does that budget range fit within your comfort level?"

Client: "Not really sure. I guess it will depend on where the other bids are priced."

Agency: "Ok. That makes sense. Getting bids is always a good idea, especially when you haven't done projects like this in the past. Just to be sure we are targeting a budget that is in the ballpark of what you are hoping for, let's compare your project to cars. If your project was a car, would you be shopping for a Ferrari or a Kia Optima? I'm not talking about the price of a Ferrari, but whether you're looking more for something with all the bells and whistles, or just something to get started and then add features in the future."

Client: "I guess we want a few high-end features now, but we don't want to spend a ton of money getting started. So, we will probably want to get the foundation in place and then add to it in the future. We are probably more like a Honda Accord than a Ferrari or a Kia Optima."

Agency: "Perfect. That sounds like a good plan. We have clients do that all the time. We'll work up some numbers, but before we go into crafting a full blown proposal, we will plan on sending you a rough estimate. Our proposals are usually 15-20 pages for something like this, but our rough estimate is just a one page document summarizing the project and giving you a price range we would expect to charge for the project. After you get your other bids and determine your budget, we would be happy to create a full proposal detailing the entire scope of the project, milestones, and so forth. Does that sound all right with you?"

Client: "That sounds great. Thank you."

As illustrated here, financial conversations can be done in a way that isn't awkward or uncomfortable, even if you have to dig deep to discover their budget. It is extremely rare that a budget conversation will require you to use all of the techniques I have outlined in this section. The client will usually divulge enough information about their budget before requiring you to send them a rough estimate.

How to Encourage Clients to Increase Their Budget

Once, I had a client who had a grand vision for a social media style website around a certain industry. The original scope was agreed upon and we began working together. As the project progressed, it became clear that the client's vision was changing and the project became much larger than our original agreement. Their budget tolerance, however, remained the same; they just wanted more features within the original budget they had allocated. Scope increases merit budget increases, and we worked together several times, increasing the budget to accommodate their changing requests. Suffice it to say, as the client began spending more and more, beyond their original budget, their intensity increased until eventually the project exploded and we discontinued working together.

There is a risk in selling a client on an increased budget. As clients begin spending bigger dollars than they have originally budgeted, there is a tendency to become hypersensitive and combative to every delivery and milestone. Every increase is scrutinized. Nothing is ever good enough. Nothing is fast enough.

As I mentioned before, nine times out of ten, when a client's budget is set, it is set. However, sometimes you will find clients who are eager to work with you and have allocated a budget that is too low due to inexperience or lack of understanding about the creative industry, rather than the objective of getting the work completed as cheaply as possible. These inexperienced clients are the type you can encourage to increase their budget commensurate with the work they are requesting. If you have determined that your client falls into this category, here are some techniques you can use to accomplish the task.

Discuss Money with Confidence

Anytime you are discussing money with your client, you must speak with confidence. This is a rule threading through every chapter of this book. Know your numbers. Speak with authority and assurance. If your client senses that you are unsure about any aspect of the financial arrangement on a project, they will lose trust in you.

Educate the Client with Your Expertise

A few days ago, someone reached out to me on LinkedIn offering to create a website for me for the low price of $185. Of course, the price was designed to hook me into a longer term maintenance or hosting agreement where they might actually make some money. I also chalked it up to evidence of the fact that someone, somewhere, will provide creative work for any budget. Developing countries are filled with designers who will work for very low costs in comparison to those who reside in more developed countries with a higher cost of living. In addition, websites like Fiverr have also created a highly competitive market for quick turn, low cost creative work. Want a five

*

Speak with confidence. If your client senses that you are unsure about any aspect of the financial arrangement on a project, they will lose confidence in you.

*

You must convince your client that increasing their budget to work with you will yield both a better result and a more pleasant experience.

dollar logo? You can get one. Hoping for a one hundred dollar website? Someone will make that budget work.

Make no mistake about it, your client can find someone to do the project for the budget they have allocated. If you want to sell your client on an increased budget, you must convince them that spending more to work with you will be better than the low cost alternatives.

Expertise is the first reason working with you will be better for your client than working with a lower cost agency. Your expertise will yield a more successful result. Sure, they can pick the lower cost designer and get a lower cost result. But if they increase their budget and choose you, the quality of the work you produce will yield a bigger return to them.

How can you convince them this is the case? Prove it by presenting case studies showing the successful results of similar projects you have completed in the past. Whenever possible, make the results numeric. You should find yourself saying things like, "After we launched the new site for our client, their traffic increased by 400% in the first two months," and, "This billboard we created led to a 200% increase in ticket sales." When you are able to provide examples like this, you will be empowered to convince clients to increase their budget and choose you for their project.

The second way to educate your client with your expertise is by showing that your processes yield a better experience. They can choose a lower end designer to produce the work for a lower cost, but they will encounter the headaches that go with the cheaper choice. Missed deadlines, poor communication, and unexecuted change requests plague the experience of low cost design work.

In order to convince your client that working with you will be a smoother and more pleasant experience than choosing a lower cost designer, you must walk them through your processes. Show them how you track milestones. Take them through the deliveries of a previous project, step by step. Do all you can to demonstrate to them that you are more organized, more experienced, and easier to work with than the low cost solution.

Finally, educate the client by walking them through the breadth of work you will do to successfully execute on their project. Describe what each design round will include. Walk them through your QA process. Show them the care and consideration you put into each phase of the project to guarantee its success.

While it may cost more to work with you, the results and experience will far exceed what they get from a creative professional who is willing to cut corners in order to work within the client's low budget. You must convince them of this fact to win the bid at a higher price than the competition.

Price Anchoring

On January 27, 2010, Steve Jobs took the stage in his customary jeans and long-sleeved black T-shirt and unveiled the very first version of the iPad. He also provided an amazing example of the sales technique known as price anchoring.

First, he spent a few minutes preparing the audience for the announcement. This time was spent on a few "tablet" related jokes along with a brief history of what lead to the creation of Apple's tablet computer. At 3 minutes and 27 seconds, the word "iPad" dropped from the top of the screen and slammed to the center with an audible thud and a cloud of dust. The audience applauded for 13 seconds. At this point, everyone in the room knew they had seen the future, and they were right.

Next, Steve Jobs spent several minutes showing slide examples of what the iPad looks like and what it does. He then spent over 40 minutes demonstrating an actual iPad.

After he had convincingly sold everybody on wanting this sparkly new Apple product, he said, "What should we price it at?" The audience laughed because they had been wondering the price for the past 40 minutes. "Well," he continued, "if you listen to the pundits, we are going to price it under a thousand dollars, which is code for $999." At this point a giant $999 filled the presentation screen.

"When we set out to develop the iPad, we not only had very ambitious technical goals, and user interface goals, but we had a very aggressive price goal. Because we want to put this in the hands of lots of people. And, just like we were able to meet or exceed our technical goals, we have met our cost goals and I am thrilled to announce to you that the iPad pricing starts, not at $999, but at just $499." A giant $499 drops from the top of the screen shattering the $999 price as the crowd cheers. Steve Jobs announces the price again, "$499. At $499 a lot of people can afford an iPad."

This is price anchoring and showmanship at its finest, courtesy of the late, great Steve Jobs. During his price discussion, the $999 price anchor sat on the screen for nearly a minute while the audience got used to the idea of a thousand dollar device.

When the $499 price dropped from the top of the screen and shattered the price anchor, the sale was complete. Everyone who planned to buy the new tablet for $999 felt like they just won $500 in the lottery and everyone who didn't think they could afford it, decided to buy. It was as if the iPad was discounted by 50% before the device was even released.

Price anchoring refers to the tendency people have to use the first price presented to make subsequent judgments. How would the crowd have reacted had Steve Jobs presented the $499 price first, and then told the audience that it was actually $999? If $499 had been used as the price anchor (the first price presented), the audience would, undoubtedly, have thought that the iPad was very expensive at $999. But, by using $999 as the price anchor and masterfully leaving it on the screen for nearly a minute, the subsequent judgment of a $499 price tag was a great deal.

In a similar way, we can use price anchoring to help our clients increase their budget to work with us. Let's say a client approaches you with an open RFP to create a website for their company. Their RFP states they have a $12,000 budget for the project. The last three websites you created comparable to the site they are requesting were all priced around $15,000. You know your cost to produce the work will be approximately $11,000, so you are not interested in doing the work for $12,000 since your profit margin will be less than 10%. You would consider doing the project for a 25% profit margin, but that would require them to increase their budget to $13,750 (i.e. this your cost of $11,000 plus a 25% profit margin).

Your conversation with the client will go something like this, "We are excited about working with you on this website. This project is a perfect fit for our agency. The last three sites we did similar to the one you are looking to create were all priced around $15,000."

You dropped the price anchor ($15,000) and you now will let it sit for a minute, like Steve Jobs, while you explain those projects.

"Each of the three projects were very successful. We helped the clients organize their content, designed the sites and completed all the programming. We continue to maintain the sites and the clients have seen an increase in traffic every month." You continue with a few more sentences while the client lets the $15,000 price settle in their head.

You then say something along the lines of, "Now, we know that your budget is only $12,000 and our past prices are too high for your current budget. However, we really want to work with you and are pretty certain that doing the site for $13,750 would work for our agency. Is there a possibility that you could increase your budget to that range?"

At this point, the client is thinking one of two things, "Excellent, they gave us a nice discount." Or, they are thinking, "I only have $12,000. I can't increase my budget with money I don't have." Either way, the price anchoring technique was successful. The client will consider increasing their budget or you will know you have made the right decision in letting them proceed with an agency that can offer a lower price (and most likely a lower quality solution).

Once you understand price anchoring you will begin to recognize it being used all over. The used car priced at $15,999 is parked next to the used car priced at $9,999. The restaurant menu will have the $39 steak right next to the grilled chicken for $14.99. They are selling the chicken all day long. Give this approach a try the next time you need to encourage a client to increase their budget.

Provide the Client with a Range of Options

Another successful technique is to provide the client with a range of options to help them visualize the benefits of increasing their budget. This technique is often referred to as price bracketing.

The classic price bracket provides three options. You see this frequently with software services that include an entry level choice, a middle of the road option, and an advanced, or pro, option. The entry level choice is designed to hook the user on the solution by providing a low cost entry point to get them using the service. The advanced option is so feature rich it either provides the business with a high profit solution for their power users, or it drives people to choose the middle of the road option, or choose, at minimum, the entry level option.

Similarly, with creative services, if a client has a budget too low to complete the work they are requesting, we can encourage them to consider a higher budget by providing a range of price options. Here's how this works.

Let's assume that your client came to you to design a new logo for their company. They have allocated a $3,000 budget and they are looking to get the main logo designed, a package of secondary logos, business cards, and a small logo usage guide. You would typically charge $6,000 for this set of services, but you know that based on your production cost, you would still have sufficient profit in the project if you charged $5,500.

Providing a client with a range of options can help them visualize the benefits of increasing their budget.

You could divide the scope of work into a few different options for the client, each with a different price point. The highest option would be the full scope of work for $5,500. The middle option could perhaps include the main logo, the secondary logos, and the business cards for $4,000. The entry level option could just be the main logo for $3,000 (their budgeted amount).

Lowest Option	Middle Option	Highest Option
Main Logo	Main Logo	Main Logo
	Secondary Logos	Secondary Logos
	Business Cards	Business Cards
		Logo Usage Guide
$3,000	**$4,000**	**$5,500**

You would then present these price brackets to your client, starting with the most expensive option in a manner similar to the following: "Thank you for letting us bid on this project. We are very excited about the prospect of working with you and know we would be able to do a great job. We usually charge $6,000 for a project like yours, which we know is out of your budget." (Boom! You drop a price anchor into the conversation prior to presenting the other options.)

You continue, "Since we are so excited about the project, we would be willing to create all of the pieces you have requested for $5,500, which is less than our typical rate. We know that is still more than your budget, so we crunched the numbers and would be willing to do the main logo, secondary logos, and business cards for $4,000, which we realize is still more than your budget. So, we would like to offer a third option at your budget amount where we would just create the main logo at $3,000. This third option should be viewed as an entry point that gets you the logo you need and then we can always create the other materials in the future."

I put more things in the middle package in an effort to highlight the benefits of choosing this package. You should also recognize the middle package is a $1,000 increase over the entry package and the high package is a $1,500 increase over the middle package. This approach makes it psychologically easier to jump from the entry level option to the middle option.

When offering a range of prices, make sure that you know your production cost for each package so that the prices you offer are each still profitable at a level fitting with your business objectives.

Create Doubt in a Competitor's Ability to Execute

Another simple technique to help a client increase their budget and choose to work with you is by creating doubt in a competitor's ability to execute on the work at the budget level the client is hoping to spend. This approach is best utilized if the client seems to have already made a decision to go with a cheaper agency.

It goes something like this, "We really would like to work with you and it is too bad that we can't make the numbers work. Just by way of advice, sometimes agencies will offer a cheap price to hook the client into the project and then when things get going, they begin sending change orders for things that you might think are in scope. So, if you are going to go with a cheaper agency, just make sure the project scope is very clearly defined. You'll want to make sure the contract defines each deliverable and how many rounds of feedback you get, and so on."

The statements above provide good advice for the client, while at the same time, they are designed to create some concern that the cheaper agency they have chosen to work with will end up sending them change orders and costing more than originally outlined. You can feel good about the approach because are you genuinely offering them beneficial counsel.

Oftentimes, I add something like, "You'll want to make sure that you are comparing apples to apples on quality, as well. If you feel the lower cost agency can provide you with high enough quality work for your budget, then from a business perspective it makes total sense to go with them."

After these two statements, the client will now dissect the competitors proposal with some concerns about future change orders and they will scrutinize the quality of design work delivered by the lower cost competitor.

With this technique, I usually end with a closing statement like, "Well, if things don't work out with the cheaper agency, give us a call. We would love to work with you."

Don't Play Games

My final piece of advice about encouraging clients to increase their budget is don't play games. There is a very fine line between salesmanship in business and game playing. Several of the recommendations I have given here are right on that line. Are they games? Are they just sales techniques? You'll have to be judge for yourself and use them as you see fit for your specific circumstances.

As for me, I prefer a straightforward business style, "Here is the price. Here is the scope. If it works with your budget, let's make something great together!" I don't find myself trying to sell clients on increasing their budget very often, but when I do, I have found success using the techniques outlined in this chapter.

Variable 03: Client Budget Worksheet

Methods for Extracting the Client's Budget for a Project

Step 01: Ask the Client

If you want to know the answer to something, ask. Designers are often timid about asking their clients for budget numbers. Don't be. Put on your grown-up pants, muster some courage, and follow this outline to ensure that you don't come across as a gold-digger.

01	**Ask a lot of questions about the project.** ____________________ ____________________ ____________________
02	**Act interested and take notes.** ____________________ ____________________ ____________________
03	**Make sure that you clearly understand the scope of the project. Restate your understanding to the client.**
04	**Ask for their budget.** "Thank you, ____________, this is all great information. I think that gives us a pretty clear picture of what you are wanting to accomplish. Is there a budget range you are shooting work within?"

Step 02:
Ask About Past Projects

If the client was unwilling to divulge their budget number using the method in Step 01, the next best method is to ask them about the pricing of past projects.

> **"What have you spent on projects similar to this in the past?"**

Step 03: Float a Price Range

If the client does not divulge what they have spent on past projects (or perhaps they haven't had experience with past projects at all), you will need to utilize a different approach. Try giving them a price range based on your experience. Be sure to pause after you float your pricing to assess their facial expression and body language.

Similar Past Projects

Project Name	Client Name	Price

Price Range to Float

$	to	$

"Our past few projects similar to this were priced between $__________ and $__________. Is that a comfortable price range for you?"

Step 04: Compare other Products

If the client is still unwilling to share their pricing tolerance with you, it is time to at least determine whether they are considering a high-end budget, a mid-range budget, or a low-end budget. This can be done by comparing brands that everyone understands. I have had the best luck using car brands as a metaphoric comparison.

"A Ford Focus and an S-Class Mercedes will both get you from point A to point B, but they are very different. They both have four wheels and an engine but the Mercedes will include all kinds of high-end features and bells and whistles that you won't find in the Ford. Are you wanting something really high-end? Or are you just looking to get started and then plan to add higher-end features later? Which type of car would your project be?"

Step 05: Send a Rough Estimate

When the client is still reluctant to share their budget using the other methods, I highly recommend you do not spend the time and energy creating a full proposal or contract for the project. Try sending them a simple, one page "rough estimate" summarizing the project scope and detailing a price range.

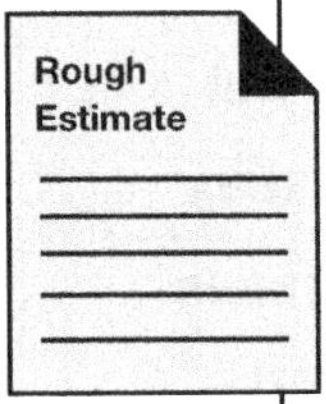

Hi Ralph!

Thank you for considering us for your project. We think our agency would be a great fit to successfully complete the work for your company.

Before we take the time to detail out the entire project scope, we thought it would be best to send you a quick estimate to make sure we are on the same page. Please see the attached PDF that contains a summary of the project as we understand it, and an estimated price range.

If this seems in harmony with your expectations, our next step would be to provide you with a full proposal detailing each aspect of the project, along with a committed price to complete the work.

Please reach out if you have any questions. I look forward to hearing from you!

Thank you!

Step 06: Determine the Client's Budget

We will use the client's budget as the final variable in our pricing spectrum as we prepare to determine our project price. In the rare case the client has still not divulged their budget, you should make your best guess for their budget number.

Variable 03: Client Budget

$

1. **Is the budget big enough for us to generate a profit if we win the project?**

   ☐ **Yes** ☐ **No**

2. **If you answered "No" to question number 1, is the budget too low due to the client's inexperience (and not as a result of them being "cheap")?**

   ☐ **Yes** ☐ **No**

If you answered "Yes" to question number 2, you may consider encouraging the client to increase their budget using the techniques found on pages 85-96.

06

CHAPTER 06

Creating the Pricing Spectrum

We now have our three variables: production cost, market value, and client budget. It is time to create our pricing spectrum and put these variables to work.

Take Time to Get Your Numbers Right

I've spent the majority of this book outlining the methods to determine your numbers for the three variables used in a pricing spectrum. Take the time to get them right. Make your calculations and analysis. Ask your client the tough questions. You are in business, it is time to run it like a business: by the numbers.

Organize Your Numbers from High to Low

Take your three variables and organize them from high to low. If the market value is the highest, it goes on top. If your production cost is second highest, it goes in the middle. If the client's budget is the lowest, it goes on the bottom.

Let's look at an example where you determined the market value of a project is $2,000, the client budget is $1,200, and your cost to produce the work is $600. Your numbers would be organized in this manner.

$2,000	**Market Value**
$1,200	**Client Budget**
$600	**Production Cost**

The high to low order varies from project to project and client to client. There are times you may find that the client's budget is the highest number and other times it may be the lowest number. It really varies for each agency, project opportunity, and client.

For example, if the client budget for a project is $5,000, the market value is $4,500, and your cost to produce the work is $2,800, your spectrum would be organized like this:

$5,000	**Client Budget**
$4,500	**Market Value**
$2,800	**Production Cost**

In some situations, a client may have a low budget that does not cover your production cost or come near the market value for a project. You still organize the pricing spectrum with the high number on top and the lowest number on bottom.

$8,500	**Market Value**
$6,500	**Production Cost**
$4,000	**Client Budget**

Choose Your Price from the Spectrum

Choosing your price requires a careful analysis of the three variables. Sometimes you will select a price close to market value and other times you may need to come in under the client's budget. Every project for every client is a little different.

In the next chapter, we will do a deep dive into the psychology of choosing a price.

07

CHAPTER 07

The Psychology of Choosing a Price

Imagine a world where every project you take on is priced to be profitable, where you intentionally decide to be just under budget to undercut the competition, and where you price projects in a way that maximizes profitability. It is time to unleash the magic of the pricing spectrum based on our three variables.

There are certain nuances in the psychology of choosing a price for your graphic design work. Scope, budgets, client expectations, expertise, availability, and the competitive landscape varies for every project request and affects our decisions on how to price our work. Before we dig in, we should discuss the psychology behind the actual numbers you should choose when you price your projects.

The Left-digit Effect vs. Whole Number Prices

Walking through the aisles of your local supermarket, you will find plenty of products with odd number prices: a gallon of milk for $2.99, a loaf of fresh baked bread for $3.99, or perhaps a small bag of chips for $1.99. For decades, products have been priced this way based on something called "the left-digit effect." The mentality behind the left-digit effect is that using a number ending in nine rather than zero changes the left most digit. For example, if a product is priced at $2.99 rather than $3.00, then there is only a difference of $.01, but the perceived price is $1.00 cheaper because the left-digit changed from a three to a two.

One could argue that most consumers are savvy enough to see through this pricing game and clearly see the $2.99 price tag as costing $3.00. Yet, I find myself using this very same tactic when I add to my collection of digital movies on my Apple account. I tell my wife that a movie was on sale for $9.99 (the exact price), rather than saying it was $10.00 (the price when rounded up by one cent). Of course, she sees through my pricing charade, but, psychologically, we all feel a tad better about the $9.99 price.

Even though this tactic is popular, there is another school of thought that consumers actually prefer round numbers in pricing. A quick online search with the terms "pricing with whole numbers" will reveal numerous articles and studies that support this concept. One such article reveals that rounded prices, like $300, encourage the consumer to purchase based on feelings, whereas irregular, non-rounded prices, like $297.50, require the consumer to make a purchase decision based on reasoning whether it is a good deal, or not. *(This Number Just Feels Right: The Impact of Roundedness of Price Numbers on Product Evaluations, Monica Wadhwa and Kuangjie Zhang, Journal of Consumer Research, Vol. 41, No. 5, February 2015, pp. 1172-1185, Published by Oxford University Press.)*

For better or worse, most businesses make marketing related decisions based on what "feels right" to them, including the decision as to which agency to hire. The goal when pricing our work is to have the clients say to themselves, "Yes, that price feels right to me."

All that being said, graphic designers are not selling eggs and I don't believe in playing games by pricing creative services with nines at the end (e.g., Get your logo design, just $5,999! Today only!)

However, based on my experience, I believe that a price of $1,750 stands a better chance of being approved than $2,000. This is not based on the belief that a client will perceive the $1,750 as actually costing $1,000 (as with left-digit pricing), but rather, clients tend to have budgets with whole numbers. If a client has a budget of $2,000 for a project and your price is $1,750, the client has a perceived victory right at the start of the project by saving some of their budget for future needs.

Additionally, in a competitive bidding situation where you are going head to head with other creative agencies or freelancers to win a project, a price of $1,750 against a client budget of $2,000 has a better chance of being lower than some of your competitor's prices simply due to the fact that you are below budget.

Mixing a little bit of the left-digit effect with the importance of honest and straightforward, whole number pricing, I propose rounding your prices based on increments proportional to the overall size of the price. Lower priced projects use lower rounded price multiples. Higher priced projects use higher rounded price multiples. Here are some guidelines to follow.

Rule 01: Above $100 and below $2,000, price your project using any multiple of $25

If your project price is above $100 and below $2,000, use any multiple of $25 for the price you present to your client.

For example, if you are pricing the design of a banner ad for one of your clients and you have determined that you should charge a price between $1,500 and $1,700 for the work. Using these guidelines, you would choose any price with a multiple of $25 since your price range is above $100 and below $2,000. This could be $1,525, $1,650, $1,675 or any other multiple of $25 within your predetermined price range. (We should avoid prices that are not multiples of $25, like $1,599 and $1,628.)

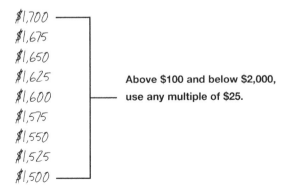

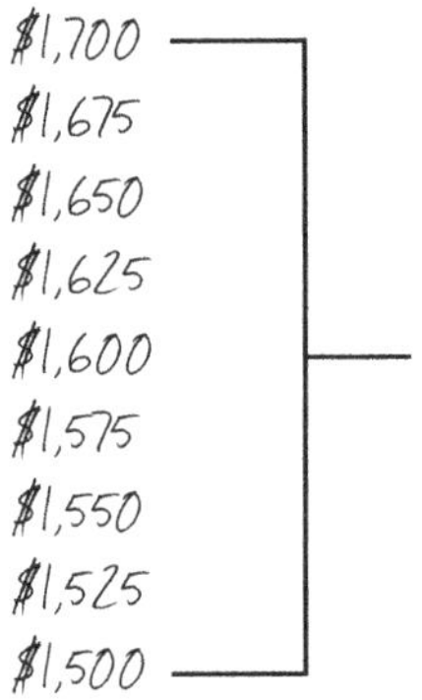

Above $100 and below $2,000, use any multiple of $25.

Rule 02: Above $2,000 and below $10,000, price your project using any multiple of $50

Let's examine the next pricing tier. If your project price is above $2,000 and below $10,000, use any multiple of $50 for your prices. Below are several examples of prices that match this recommendation.

Using these guidelines, if you have decided to charge your client between $3,000 and $3,500 for the design of a tri-fold brochure, you would choose any number that has a multiple of $50 for your final price. For example, $3,250, $3,350, $3,400 or any other multiple of $50. (You would not choose $3,399, $3,325, $3,407 or any other number that is not a multiple of $50.)

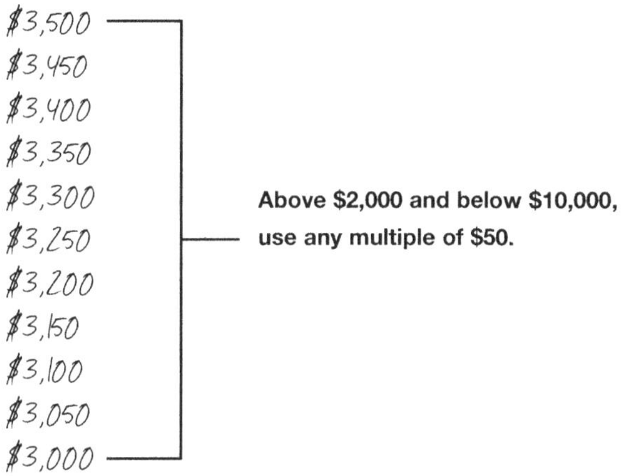

Most businesses make marketing related decisions based on what feels right to them. The goal when pricing our work is to have the clients say to themselves, "Yes, that price feels right to me."

Rule 03: Above $10,000, price your project using any multiple of $250

Finally, if your project price is above $10,000, use any multiple of $250 for your prices.

With this standard as your guide, if you were pricing a website project in a range between $22,000 and $25,000, you would choose any price that is a multiple of $250. For example, a final price of $22,250, $23,000, or $24,500 would be an appropriate choice. (You would not choose $23,225, $24,999, $22,777 or $22,889 because they are not multiples of $250.)

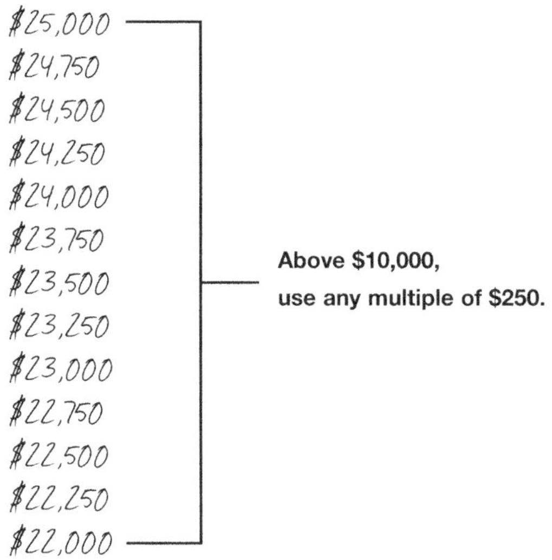

Much of our success comes from building a relationship of trust with our clients. Being straightforward in your pricing decisions is a great step toward building the right relationship with your customer.

Now that we know how to build our pricing spectrum and what numbers we should choose based on certain pricing thresholds, let's explore some real world scenarios to put everything we have learned so far into practice. You will reference these scenarios when pricing your projects.

12
Pricing Spectrum Scenarios

PRICING SPECTRUM

Scenario 01

Desperate for Work

Your Situation:

You have hit a dry spell in workload and feel the start of freelancer panic setting in. You really need this project to generate some necessary income.

The Pricing Spectrum:

You have determined the market value for the work is $2,000. The client's budget is $1,200 and your estimated cost to produce the work is $600.

$2,000	Market Value
$1,200	Client Budget
$600	Production Cost

Recommendation:

Bid the project using your production cost as the most important variable and add a fair profit margin. In this example, I would recommend pricing the work at $800. This price is your production cost of $600 plus a 30% markup ($600 x 0.30 = $180, then add back your production cost of $600 = $780, which we round up to $800). By being considerably under budget, you increase your odds of beating out any competing bidders but you still have a decent profit margin for the work.

You could consider adding more profit to the project by increasing your price to $825, $850, or $900. You might even bid a tad higher than that, as long as you don't feel like you are compromising your chance of receiving a green light for the work you desperately need.

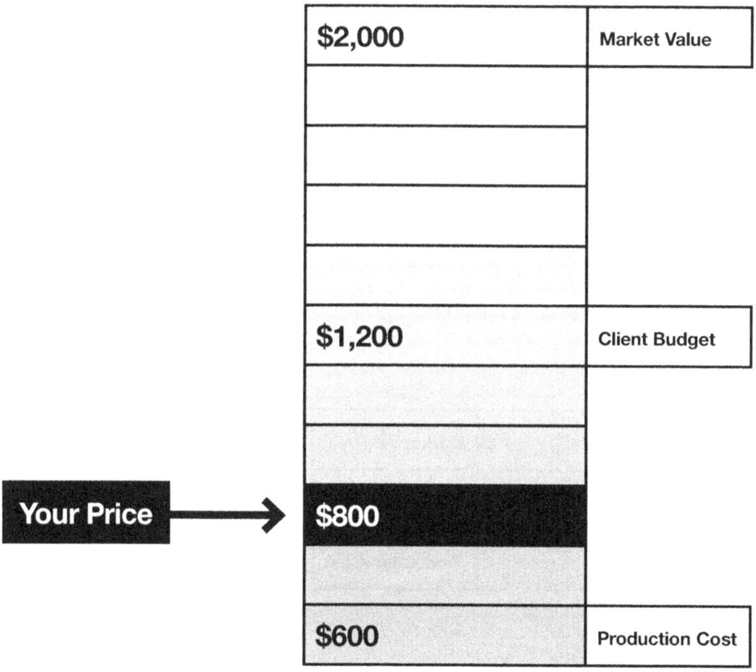

PRICING SPECTRUM

Scenario 02

Yes, for the Right Price

Your Situation:

Your workload is pretty heavy, but for the right price, you would be willing to work longer days or some weekend hours.

The Pricing Spectrum:

You have determined the market value for the work is $3,000. The client's budget is $2,500 and your estimated cost to produce the work is $1,200.

$3,000	Market Value
$2,500	Client Budget
$1,200	Production Cost

Recommendation:

Bid the project near the client's budget. If you are in a competitive bidding situation, consider $2,400 to be just under the client's budget. Otherwise, I recommend that you price your project at $2,500. If you win it, great, more work with a sizable profit margin! If you don't win it, great, you are busy and would have had to cram it in anyway.

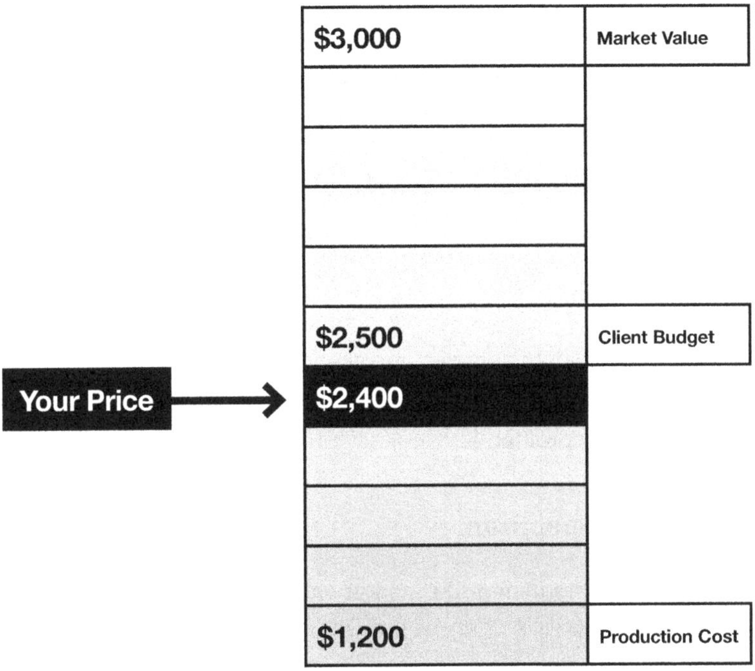

PRICING SPECTRUM

Scenario 03

Slammed but Ambitious

Your Situation:

You're completely slammed and already sacrificing sleep for work. However, you are a hungry freelancer and would take on more if the project was very profitable.

The Pricing Spectrum:

You have determined the market value for the work is $2,000. The client's budget is $1,500 and your estimated cost to produce the work is $900.

$2,000	Market Value
$1,500	Client Budget
$900	Production Cost

Recommendation:

Bid the project near the market value and rely on your ability to sell the client on increasing their budget. In this situation, I would recommend bidding the project around $1,800. You are still below market value, so you should not feel bad about your price and based on your cost of $900, you have a 100% markup on the work.

When you bid above the client's budget, you are at great risk of not winning the project. However, as busy as you are, losing out is not necessarily a bad thing.

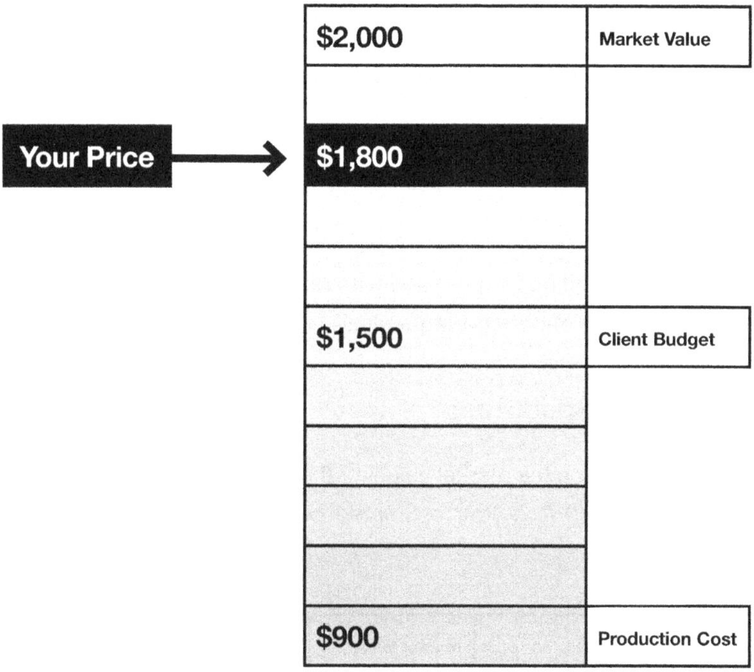

PRICING SPECTRUM

Scenario 04

Difficult Client

Your Situation:

During your discovery meetings, your Spidey-sense was tingling. This may be a difficult client filled with indecision, a challenging personality, or a lot of change requests.

The Pricing Spectrum:

You determine the market value for the work is $4,000. The client's budget is $3,000 and your estimated cost to produce the work is $2,500.

$4,000	Market Value
$3,500	Client Budget
$2,500	Production Cost

Recommendation:

Challenging clients usually require more budget than amiable clients. If you bid the project too low, there is significant risk that you won't be profitable as you navigate extra changes and client indecision. Additionally, you are justified in charging more to a client with a difficult personality to help cover the emotional cost of working with them.

In these situations, I recommend that you bid the project at (or above) the market value of $4,000. This leaves plenty of padding in your price to help you navigate the extra hassle required trying to please a potentially difficult client.

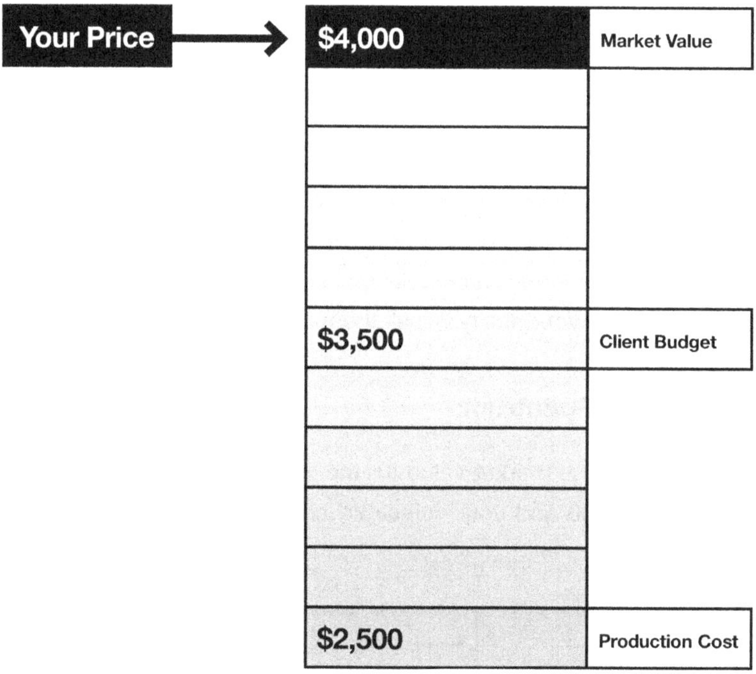

PRICING SPECTRUM

Scenario 05

Experience Merits Money

Your Situation:

You have been a successful designer for a long time. You understand your numbers and know you can out produce the competition in both quality and turnaround time. Although the client doesn't appear to be difficult, your skills and experience merit a higher price and you are confident in your ability to sell them on it.

The Pricing Spectrum:

You know the market value for the work is $6,000. The client's budget is $4,500 and your estimated cost to produce the work is $3,000.

$6,000	**Market Value**
$4,500	**Client Budget**
$3,000	**Production Cost**

Recommendation:

Bid the project at market value and make sure your proposal clearly articulates your experience and the value of the work you will produce. Be sure to include related case studies highlighting the return on investment of your past work.

In this scenario, you will be relying on your ability to sell yourself to such a degree that your client will look to increase their budget to work with you.

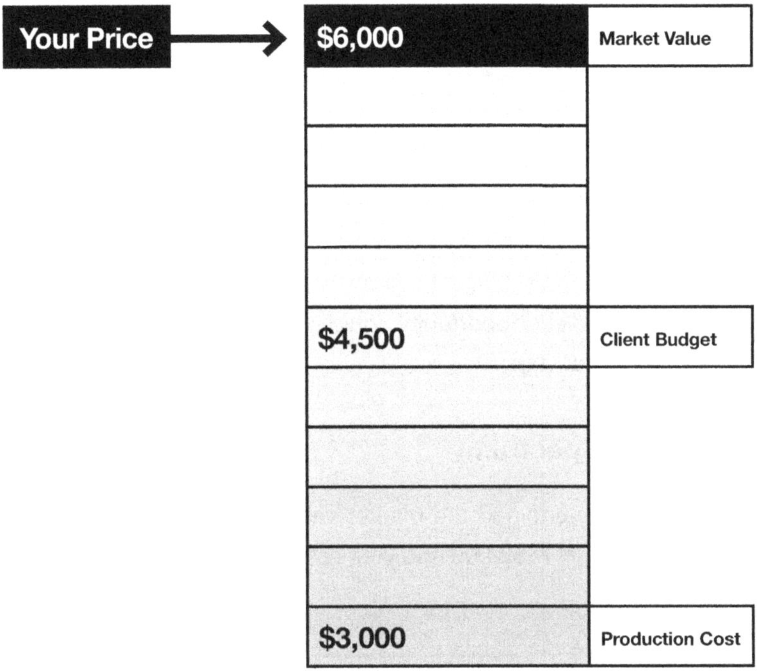

PRICING SPECTRUM

Scenario 06

Trying to Grow

Your Situation:

You are currently trying to grow your business and land new clients. Every project opportunity could potentially grow into a long-term client relationship.

The Pricing Spectrum:

You have determined the market value for the work is $2,500. The client's budget is $2,000 and your estimated cost to produce the work is $1,250.

$2,500	**Market Value**
$2,000	**Client Budget**
$1,250	**Production Cost**

Recommendation:

Bid the project at a comfortable profitable margin, but come in under the client's budget. The client should respond with enthusiasm because they are saving budget money and you have an opportunity to show off your skills in an effort to land additional future work.

Be careful to not come in too low and sacrifice a healthy profit margin. You don't want to train a long-term client to expect a great deal on every project. In this scenario, I would recommend $1,750. This price is your cost plus a decent profit margin, while still lower than the client's budget.

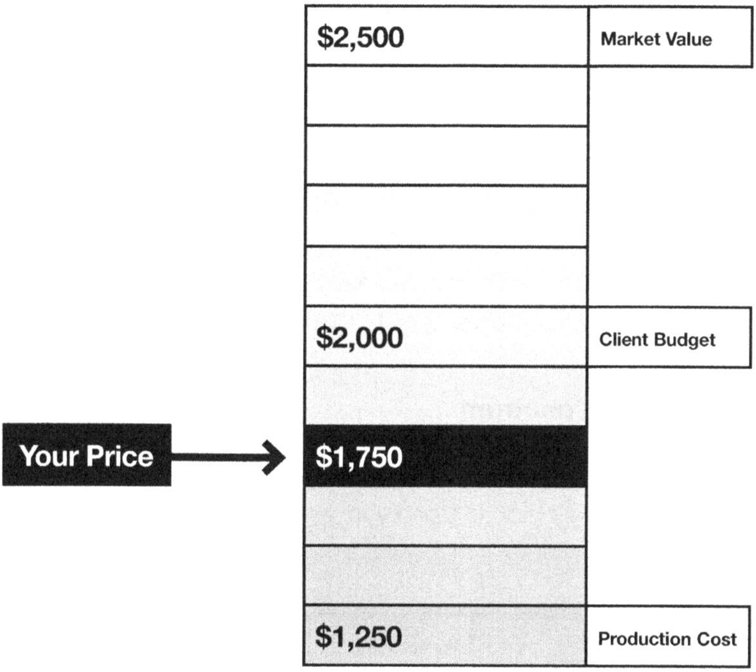

PRICING SPECTRUM

Scenario 07

Heavy Competition

Your Situation:

Your potential client sent out a detailed request for proposal (RFP). The RFP contains the scope of the project, along with the client's budget. The client also disclosed that they are having multiple agencies (or creative freelancers) bid on the project.

The Pricing Spectrum:

You have determined the market value for the work is $7,500. The client's budget is $6,000 and your estimated cost to produce the work is $4,500.

$7,500	**Market Value**
$6,000	**Client Budget**
$4,500	**Production Cost**

Recommendation:

Beat the competition on price and come in under budget. It is safe to assume at least a few of the other bidders will undercut the proposed budget as well. In a world where so many clients make their selection based on quality, speed to produce the work, and price, there is too much risk being the high bidder in a competitive bidding situation. If quality and time are equal across all of the bids and you are the high price, you will likely be eliminated. Don't take the risk.

Come in at $5,500. You still have a high profit margin on the project and you are nearly 10% below the client's budget. When all bidders know the budget, the competitive prices are frequently at, or near, the budget amount. To win on price, you must come in lower.

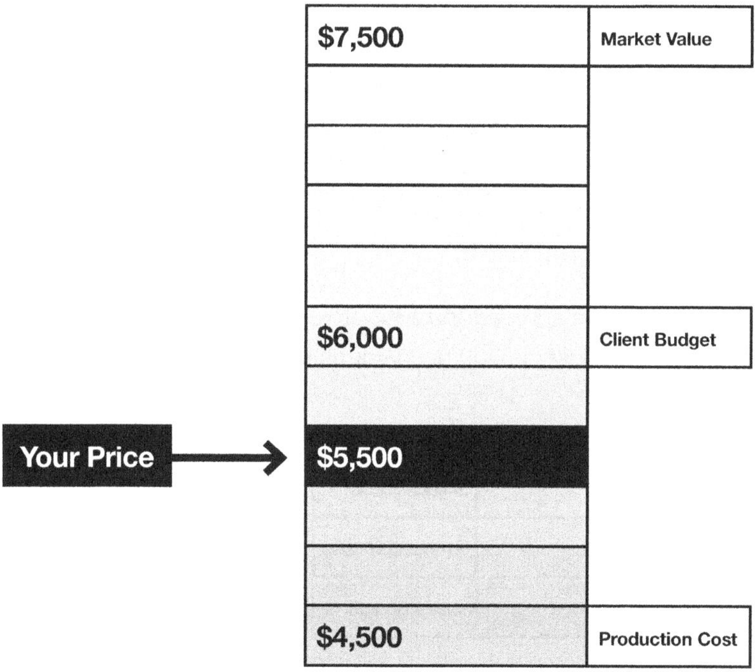

PRICING SPECTRUM

Scenario 08

Budget too Low

Your Situation:

You meet with a new client and do an analysis of their request. After plotting your variables, you find the client's budget is too low for the project.

The Pricing Spectrum:

You have determined the market value for the work is $1,500. The client's budget is $400 and your estimated cost to produce the work is $600.

$1,500	**Market Value**
$600	**Production Cost**
$400	**Client Budget**

Recommendation:

Don't bid on the project as currently outlined. The client's budget is too low for you to generate a profit. You should never take on a project that is guaranteed to be unprofitable. Some agencies will try to convince themselves that any cashflow is better than no cashflow and attempt to work within the low budget. Financial hardships await those who embrace this logic. Don't do it.

In addition to the profitability issues, the client's budget is far below market value which is unfair to the industry.

When the client's budget is lower than your production cost, there are only two ways you can make the project work. First, you can collaborate with the client to reduce the scope of the project to fit within their budget. Second, you can discuss the potential of increasing the budget using the techniques I outlined on pages 85-96.

In this situation, I would gracefully decline the project and start the conversation about next steps by telling the client, "Thank you for considering our agency for your project. After reviewing the scope and assessing our cost to produce the work, we have determined that we are probably not a good fit for the project based on the current scope and the budget you have allocated. If you are open to considering modifying the scope of the project or increasing your budget, we would love to discuss some ideas with you."

PRICING SPECTRUM

Scenario 09

Big Budget

Your Situation:

Your potential client unveils their budget and you are surprised to find that it is higher than both the market value and your cost to produce the work.

The Pricing Spectrum:

You have determined the client's budget is $10,000. The competitive market value is $7,000 and your estimated cost to produce the work is $4,000.

$10,000	**Client Budget**
$7,000	**Market Value**
$4,000	**Production Cost**

Recommendation:

Before you shout for joy, it is time to do a little soul searching. Do you really understand the scope of the project? Is it much bigger than you think? Does your client really understand the scope of the project? Are they expecting something much bigger than you are thinking?

If you do an honest assessment of those questions and still feel confident in bidding on the project, you may have just struck gold. These are the dream opportunities that come around from time to time. Congratulations! Big budget. Big project. Big profit opportunity. Let's discuss where to price your work.

If your price is too far below their budget, you are at risk of the client becoming concerned that you don't understand the scope of the project. If you bid it too far over market value, then you are at risk of feeling like you are price gouging your client. The happy medium is to hit somewhere below their budget and above market value. In this case, $8,500 would be a number to consider.

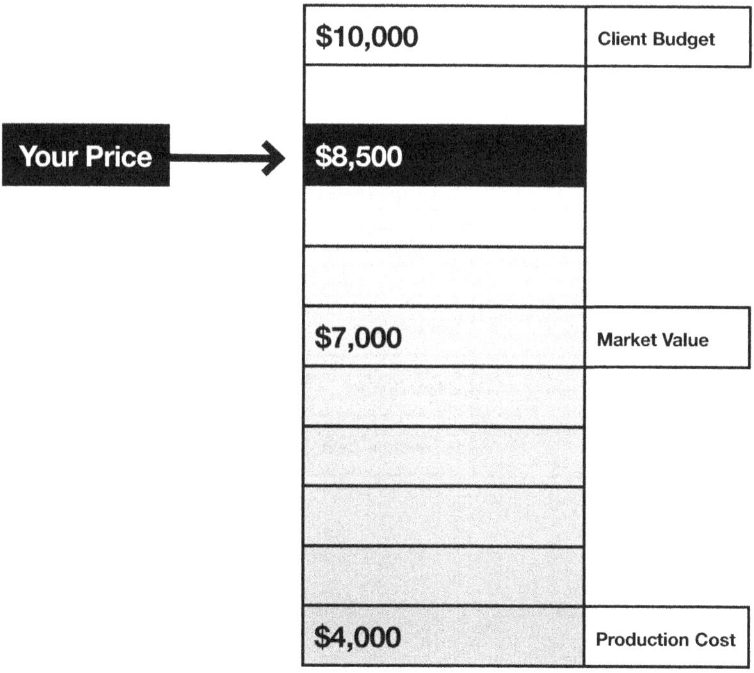

PRICING SPECTRUM

Scenario 10

Saving a Relationship

Your Situation:

Your past projects with this client have been successful, but for some reason, the last project (or your current project) has gone awry. Your client is frustrated and you are trying to make things right.

The Pricing Spectrum:

You have determined the market value for the work is $15,000. The client's budget is $12,000 and your estimated cost to produce the work is $8,000.

$15,000	**Market Value**
$12,000	**Client Budget**
$8,000	**Production Cost**

Recommendation:

If you survive in the creative industry long enough, you will eventually end up on the ugly side of a strained relationship. Perhaps the client's frustrations are your fault, or maybe all the blame falls on them. Regardless of who caused the problems, if you are still interested in working with the client, you can try to get the relationship back on track.

I added this scenario to the book merely as an opportunity to highlight the fact that many designers will take a financial loss when trying to rectify a relationship with a frustrated client. As a breed, creative people are notorious people pleasers, sometimes at any cost.

I recommend, as a gesture of good faith toward rectifying the relationship, that you price the project near your production cost, but **NEVER go lower than your production cost**. In nearly every situation, you are better off letting the client walk away mad rather than absorbing a financial loss to your business.

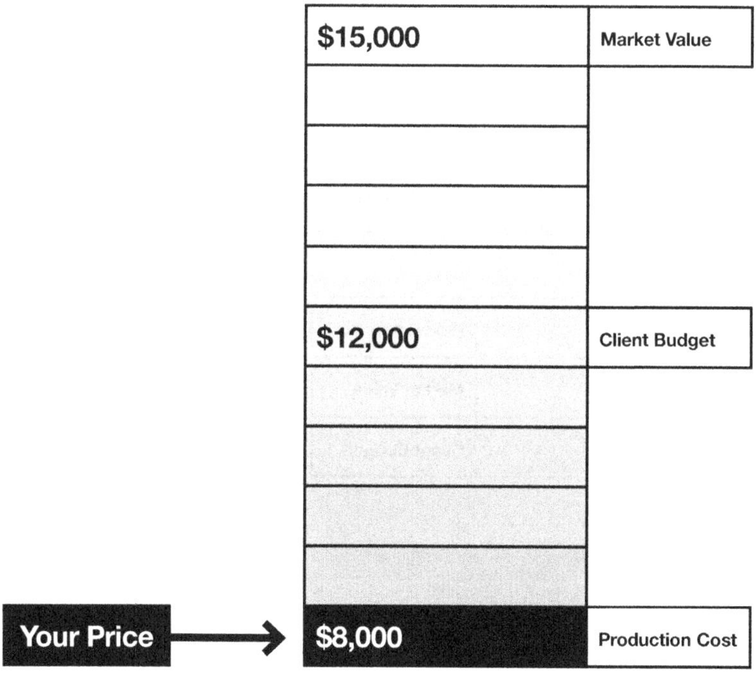

PRICING SPECTRUM

Scenario 11

Production Cost too High

Your Situation:

After careful analysis you find that your cost to produce the requested work is higher than both the market value and the client's budget.

The Pricing Spectrum:

You have determined your production cost is $7,500. The market value is $5,500 and the client's budget is $5,000.

$7,500	Production Cost
$5,500	Market Value
$5,000	Client Budget

Recommendation:

Don't bid on the project. This is a concerning place to be in. If your cost was only higher than the client's budget, then you could just chalk it up to the client being cheap. However, since your cost is also higher than the market value of the work, you need to do some analysis of your production processes and reassess how you can become competitive in the marketplace.

The problem we find in this scenario happened to a lot of agencies during the early 2010's. Until that time, three to five page brochure websites could command a high price because all of the projects included custom design and custom programming. When tools like pre-coded Wordpress Themes, Squarespace, and Wix began to gain market share, many small agencies and freelancers began producing nicely designed brochure websites without all of the customization that was previously required.

The agencies of this new era could produce the work at a lower cost and began charging cheaper prices to clients to win projects. As a result, the market value (i.e. the expected cost, not the value the site provides to the client) went down. The agencies that continued to do everything completely custom began losing out on the brochure website projects; because their cost to produce the work exceeded both the client's budget and market value. This is the type of thing you should be analyzing if your production cost is the highest in the spectrum.

Analyze your production processes and the scope of the project. Did the industry start doing things differently while you weren't paying attention? Can you change your processes to produce the work faster and become competitive at lower prices? Are there more questions you need to ask the client to ensure you fully understand the project scope? Can you work with the client to reduce the scope and come in closer to their budget?

After you do the necessary analysis, if your production costs remain higher than the market value and budget, it is likely time to pass on the project. As I have stated before, never do work that is guaranteed to be unprofitable. If you are completing work for your client at a financial loss, you are losing money; you are investing in the client's project, and, if left unchecked, you may put your business in jeopardy.

Be honest and upfront with the client, "Sorry, we have reviewed the scope of work and we just cannot produce it within the budget you are hoping to hit. We'll have to pass on this project but would love to be considered for future work."

*

Never take on a project that is guaranteed to be unprofitable. Never.

PRICING SPECTRUM

Scenario 12

Creative Superhero

Your Situation:

The final scenario worth mentioning is you are one of the lucky few designers or agencies that can command your price regardless of your production cost, market value, or client budget. Perhaps your reputation attracts clients who will pay whatever it takes to work with you. Maybe your work quality is so far superior to that of the competition, the client will choose you no matter what the cost. Or perchance, you are independently wealthy and only interested in working on a few select projects. Regardless of the reason, congratulations! You are a Creative Superhero! Charge whatever you want and don't ever feel bad about your high degree of profitability.

*

Never feel bad about earning a sizable profit on your projects just because you love what you do for a living and you're good at it.

Pricing Spectrum Worksheet Sample

Follow these steps to determine prices for your projects. I'll begin by walking you through each step and then give you several blank pricing spectrums for you to use on some of your projects. Let's do this!

Step 01:

Use the methods taught in this book to determine the number for each of the three variables: production cost, market value, and client budget. Organize your variables from highest to lowest.

$ *6,000* ← Place the variable with the highest value here. For example, if you have determined the market value is higher than both the client budget and production cost, then you would place the market value price here and write "Market Value" in the space below.

Variable: *Market Value*

$ *4,400* ← The second highest priced variable is placed here. Define the variable in the space below the value box (i.e. production cost, market value, or client budget).

Variable: *Client Budget*

$ *2,800* ← Write the lowest priced variable here, and again, define it in the space below.

Variable: *Production Cost*

Step 02:

Transpose the three variables onto the empty spectrum. Add your variable prices to the white boxes in the left column and add the variable name to the white boxes in right column. Your highest variable goes on top, the middle variable below it, and the lowest variable on the bottom.

$ 6,000	Variable: Market Value
$ 4,400	Variable: Client Budget
$ 2,800	Variable: Production Cost

Step 03 (Example 1):

Fill in the gray boxes with potential price options in between the variables above and below it. For example, if the variable above the gray box section is $6,000 and the variable below the gray box section is $4,400, you would fill in the gray boxes with a range of numbers starting just above $4,400 going up to a number just below $6,000, as seen in the example below.

$ 6,000	Variable: Market Value
5,800	
5,650	
5,400	
5,200	
5,000	
4,800	
4,600	
$ 4,400	Variable: Client Budget
4,250	
4,000	
3,750	
3,600	
3,450	
3,200	
3,000	
$ 2,800	Variable: Production Cost

Step 03 (Example 2):

The gray box sections don't need to be a systematic sequence of numbers equal in their range (i.e. 400, 600, 800, 1000). More importantly, the gray box sections should be filled with numbers that could be potential choices of where you may want to price your work. Feel free to skip numbers that would normally be in your sequence as in the example below.

$ 16,000	Variable: Market Value
15,500	
15,000	
14,500	
14,250	
13,000	
12,500	
12,250	
$ 12,000	Variable: Client Budget
11,750	
11,500	
11,250	
10,500	
10,000	
9,750	
9,500	
$ 9,000	Variable: Production Cost

Step 04:

Review the twelve pricing spectrum scenarios I provided earlier in this chapter. Which of the scenarios best fits your current situation?

☐	01	**Desperate for Work:** You are in desperate need of landing more work (pg. 114).
☐	02	**Yes, for the Right Price:** You are busy, but could fit in another project for the right price (pg. 116).
☐	03	**Slammed but Ambitious:** You have a ton of work and would only take on the project if it is highly profitable (pg. 118).
☐	04	**Difficult Client:** The client shows signs that they might be a challenge (pg. 120).
☐	05	**Experience Merits Money:** Your experience and quality merit higher prices (pg. 122).
☐	06	**Trying to Grow:** You are trying to grow your business and expand your client base (pg. 124).
X	07	**Heavy Competition:** You are competing against other creatives and everyone knows the budget (pg. 126).
☐	08	**Budget too Low:** The client's budget is lower than both the market value and your production cost (pg. 128).
☐	09	**Big Budget:** The client's budget is higher than both the market value and your production cost (pg. 130).
☐	10	**Saving a Relationship:** You are trying to salvage a strained relationship with an existing client (pg. 132).
☐	11	**Production Cost too High:** Your production cost is higher than both the market value and the client's budget (pg. 134).
☐	12	**Creative Superhero:** You set your price and the client can take it or leave it (pg. 138).

Step 05:

Based upon the recommendations that relate to your current situation, what are a few prices you should consider for your final project price? This is the step where you begin having an inner dialogue about the pros and cons of pricing your work at certain prices?

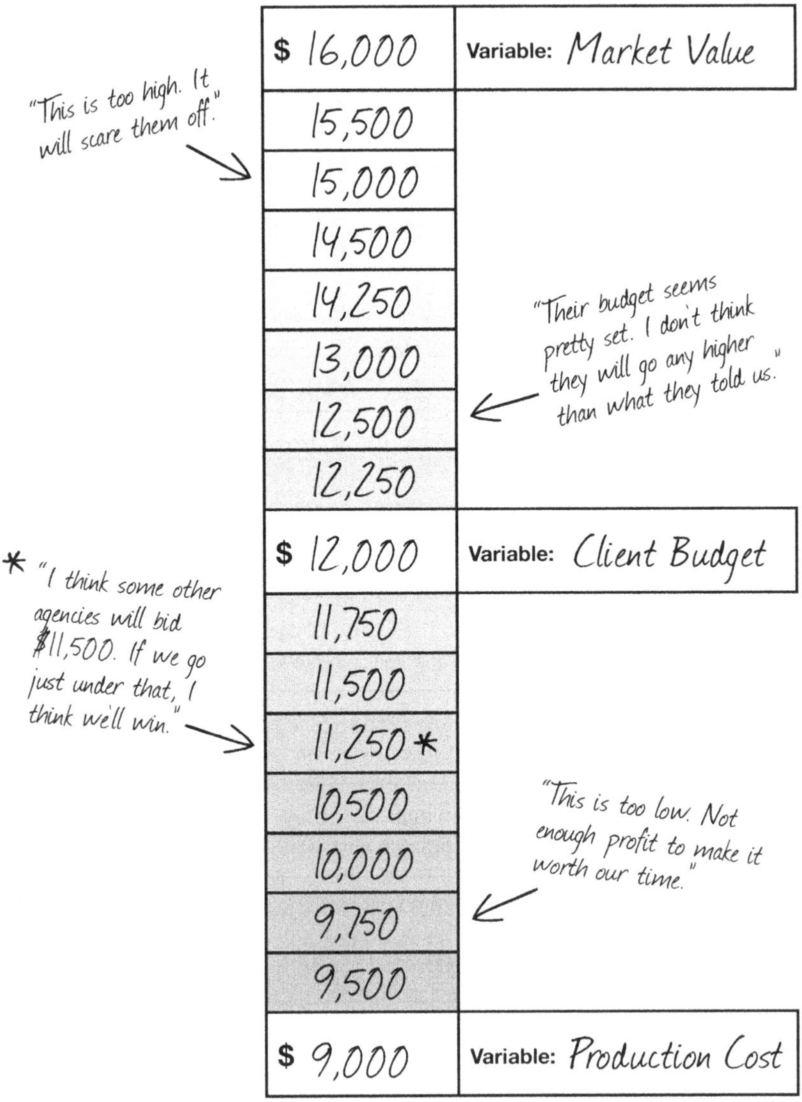
$ 16,000
Variable: Market Value
"This is too high. It will scare them off."
15,500
15,000
14,500
14,250
"Their budget seems pretty set. I don't think they will go any higher than what they told us."
13,000
12,500
12,250
$ 12,000
Variable: Client Budget
* "I think some other agencies will bid $11,500. If we go just under that, I think we'll win."
11,750
11,500
11,250 *
"This is too low. Not enough profit to make it worth our time."
10,500
10,000
9,750
9,500
$ 9,000
Variable: Production Cost

Step 06:

At this point you have done your due diligence. You have calculated your production cost. You have researched the market value of the work your client is requesting. You have extracted their budget and you have considered the current situation of your business. It is time to choose a price!

Your Project Price

$ 11,250

Step 07:

After you have selected your price, you can confirm your choice by asking yourself the following questions that relate to each of the variables we have discussed in this book.

[X] **Production Cost Variable Question**
Am I comfortable with the amount of profit I have factored into my price?

[X] **Market Value Variable Question**
Is my price in harmony with what other creative professionals like me are charging for this type of work?

[X] **Client Budget Variable Question**
Is my price in a range that my client will approve?

If you are comfortable with your answers to these questions, you are ready to create a proposal and present your price to your client.

*

Am I comfortable with the amount of profit I have factored into my price?

Is my price in harmony with what other creative professionals like me are charging for this type of work?

Is my price in a range that my client will approve?

Blank Pricing Spectrum Worksheets

Use the blank pricing spectrums on the following pages to determine prices for a few of your projects.

Pricing Spectrum

Project Name:	
Client Name:	
Date:	

☐	**01**	Identify the value of each variable: production cost, market value, and client budget.
☐	**02**	Organize the variables from highest to lowest.
☐	**03**	Fill in the gray boxes with potential prices that are in between the variables above and below.
☐	**04**	Review the twelve pricing scenarios and identify which one fits your current situation (pgs. 113-138, 145).
☐	**05**	Choose a few prices on the spectrum that you're considering for your final price. Have some inner dialogue about the pros and cons of each price option.
☐	**06**	Choose your final price and verify your price using the questions below.

	Price Verification Questions
☐	**PRODUCTION COST:** Am I comfortable with the amount of profit I have factored into my price?
☐	**MARKET VALUE:** Is my price in harmony with what other creative professionals like me are charging for this type of work?
☐	**CLIENT BUDGET:** Is my price in a range that my client will approve?

$	Variable:
$	Variable:
$	Variable:

Your Project Price

$

Pricing Spectrum

Project Name:	
Client Name:	
Date:	

☐	**01**	Identify the value of each variable: production cost, market value, and client budget.
☐	**02**	Organize the variables from highest to lowest.
☐	**03**	Fill in the gray boxes with potential prices that are in between the variables above and below.
☐	**04**	Review the twelve pricing scenarios and identify which one fits your current situation (pgs. 113-138, 145).
☐	**05**	Choose a few prices on the spectrum that you're considering for your final price. Have some inner dialogue about the pros and cons of each price option.
☐	**06**	Choose your final price and verify your price using the questions below.

	Price Verification Questions
☐	**PRODUCTION COST:** Am I comfortable with the amount of profit I have factored into my price?
☐	**MARKET VALUE:** Is my price in harmony with what other creative professionals like me are charging for this type of work?
☐	**CLIENT BUDGET:** Is my price in a range that my client will approve?

$	Variable:
$	Variable:
$	Variable:

Your Project Price

$

Pricing Spectrum

Project Name:	
Client Name:	
Date:	

☐	**01**	Identify the value of each variable: production cost, market value, and client budget.
☐	**02**	Organize the variables from highest to lowest.
☐	**03**	Fill in the gray boxes with potential prices that are in between the variables above and below.
☐	**04**	Review the twelve pricing scenarios and identify which one fits your current situation (pgs. 113-138, 145).
☐	**05**	Choose a few prices on the spectrum that you're considering for your final price. Have some inner dialogue about the pros and cons of each price option.
☐	**06**	Choose your final price and verify your price using the questions below.

	Price Verification Questions
☐	**PRODUCTION COST:** Am I comfortable with the amount of profit I have factored into my price?
☐	**MARKET VALUE:** Is my price in harmony with what other creative professionals like me are charging for this type of work?
☐	**CLIENT BUDGET:** Is my price in a range that my client will approve?

$	Variable:
$	Variable:
$	Variable:

Your Project Price

$

Pricing Spectrum

Project Name:	
Client Name:	
Date:	

☐	**01**	Identify the value of each variable: production cost, market value, and client budget.
☐	**02**	Organize the variables from highest to lowest.
☐	**03**	Fill in the gray boxes with potential prices that are in between the variables above and below.
☐	**04**	Review the twelve pricing scenarios and identify which one fits your current situation (pgs. 113-138, 145).
☐	**05**	Choose a few prices on the spectrum that you're considering for your final price. Have some inner dialogue about the pros and cons of each price option.
☐	**06**	Choose your final price and verify your price using the questions below.

	Price Verification Questions
☐	**PRODUCTION COST:** Am I comfortable with the amount of profit I have factored into my price?
☐	**MARKET VALUE:** Is my price in harmony with what other creative professionals like me are charging for this type of work?
☐	**CLIENT BUDGET:** Is my price in a range that my client will approve?

$	Variable:
$	Variable:
$	Variable:

Your Project Price

$

Pricing Spectrum

Project Name:	
Client Name:	
Date:	

☐	**01**	Identify the value of each variable: production cost, market value, and client budget.
☐	**02**	Organize the variables from highest to lowest.
☐	**03**	Fill in the gray boxes with potential prices that are in between the variables above and below.
☐	**04**	Review the twelve pricing scenarios and identify which one fits your current situation (pgs. 113-138, 145).
☐	**05**	Choose a few prices on the spectrum that you're considering for your final price. Have some inner dialogue about the pros and cons of each price option.
☐	**06**	Choose your final price and verify your price using the questions below.

	Price Verification Questions
☐	**PRODUCTION COST:** Am I comfortable with the amount of profit I have factored into my price?
☐	**MARKET VALUE:** Is my price in harmony with what other creative professionals like me are charging for this type of work?
☐	**CLIENT BUDGET:** Is my price in a range that my client will approve?

$	Variable:
$	Variable:
$	Variable:

Your Project Price

$

Pricing Spectrum

Project Name:	
Client Name:	
Date:	

☐	**01**	Identify the value of each variable: production cost, market value, and client budget.
☐	**02**	Organize the variables from highest to lowest.
☐	**03**	Fill in the gray boxes with potential prices that are in between the variables above and below.
☐	**04**	Review the twelve pricing scenarios and identify which one fits your current situation (pgs. 113-138, 145).
☐	**05**	Choose a few prices on the spectrum that you're considering for your final price. Have some inner dialogue about the pros and cons of each price option.
☐	**06**	Choose your final price and verify your price using the questions below.

	Price Verification Questions
☐	**PRODUCTION COST:** Am I comfortable with the amount of profit I have factored into my price?
☐	**MARKET VALUE:** Is my price in harmony with what other creative professionals like me are charging for this type of work?
☐	**CLIENT BUDGET:** Is my price in a range that my client will approve?

$	Variable:
$	Variable:
$	Variable:

Your Project Price

$

Pricing Spectrum

Project Name:	
Client Name:	
Date:	

☐	**01**	Identify the value of each variable: production cost, market value, and client budget.
☐	**02**	Organize the variables from highest to lowest.
☐	**03**	Fill in the gray boxes with potential prices that are in between the variables above and below.
☐	**04**	Review the twelve pricing scenarios and identify which one fits your current situation (pgs. 113-138, 145).
☐	**05**	Choose a few prices on the spectrum that you're considering for your final price. Have some inner dialogue about the pros and cons of each price option.
☐	**06**	Choose your final price and verify your price using the questions below.

	Price Verification Questions
☐	**PRODUCTION COST:** Am I comfortable with the amount of profit I have factored into my price?
☐	**MARKET VALUE:** Is my price in harmony with what other creative professionals like me are charging for this type of work?
☐	**CLIENT BUDGET:** Is my price in a range that my client will approve?

$	Variable:
$	Variable:
$	Variable:

Your Project Price

$

08

CHAPTER 08

Calculating Your Billable Hourly Rate

Although this book focuses on fixed bid style pricing, there are a few additional ways to price work for your clients, one of which is charging a billable hourly rate.

I recommend you **only charge clients based upon a billable hourly rate when you provide services that cannot be completed under a fixed bid agreement**. These types of services include, but are not limited to:

- Extra rounds of changes on a project
- Maintenance requests for digital projects
- Simple design changes
- Minor content updates
- Debugging code

Trading Time for Money Penalizes You

Trading time for money (i.e. charging your clients by the hour) is the least profitable way to price your work because it eliminates the value of the work you produce and penalizes you for working quickly. When charging a client based upon an hourly rate, the faster you complete the work, the less money you make.

On the other hand, properly scoping and providing fixed bid prices allows you to factor both market value and the client's budget into your price. Perhaps best of all, in contrast to charging your client by the hour, a fixed bid price rewards you for working quickly by increasing the financial return on your time.

A Method to the Hourly Madness

All of that being said, many clients will ask for your hourly rate, and you should know how to calculate it. **Simply stated, your billable hourly rate is your hourly burn rate with the addition of profit.**

Profit margins vary wildly from business to business. I have been told that many agencies operate at very thin profit margins, as low as 1 or 2%. My agency, Riser, ran at a 31% average annual profit margin over our lifespan. The publicly traded "mega-agencies" typically report profit margins between 5 and 10%. Mid-sized agencies may average 15 or 20% margins and some agencies could have a 50% margin or higher. A well-seasoned freelancer working from their home office with very little overhead cost could easily have a 100-200%+ markup on their hourly burn rate. The industry profit margin is really all over the place with no set standard.

Now you may be thinking, "So, how much profit should I add to my cost when calculating my billable hourly rate?" Good question.

The long answer to this question: you should consider your production cost (the amount you need to charge to cover your costs), the market value (what other people similar to you are charging), and the client budget (the amount the client has to spend on creative services). The short answer, your billable hourly rate should include as much profit as your clients will approve.

If your hourly burn rate is $30, but your clients will pay $150 per hour for your services (a 500% markup), have no concern charging it. After all, as we discussed in chapter four, the market value of a product or service is equal to the amount someone is willing to pay. If your clients will pay it, you can charge it. That is your market value.

You really just need to pick a profit margin percentage that is comfortable to you; this percentage should start, in my opinion, with at least a 20 to 30% profit margin and go up from there. You are not price gouging your customer if you decide that your profit margin should be 100%+ higher than your hourly burn rate. If you have the expertise to provide value to your customer and your customer will green light work at a higher hourly rate, then charge it! After all, you are in business to make a profit.

*

Your billable hourly rate should include as much profit as your clients will approve.

*

Every project that can be bid at a fixed price, should be.

Billable Hourly Rate Formula

It's probably impossible to eliminate every scenario that may require you to charge your client based upon an hourly rate, therefore, it is important to know how to calculate it.

Here is the formula: multiply your hourly burn rate by your desired profit margin percentage to calculate your hourly profit, then add the profit back into the hourly burn rate. The two step process and formulas look like this:

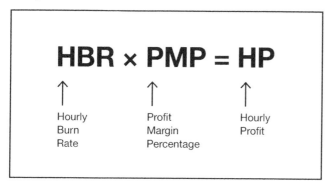

Step 01:

$$\mathbf{HBR \times PMP = HP}$$

HBR	PMP	HP
↑ Hourly Burn Rate	↑ Profit Margin Percentage	↑ Hourly Profit

Step 02:

$$\mathbf{HP + HBR = BHR}$$

HP	HBR	BHR
↑ Hourly Profit	↑ Hourly Burn Rate	↑ Billable Hourly Rate

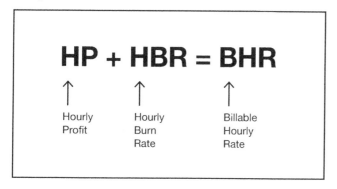

Let's look at some examples of this formula in action to help you see how it works.

Example 01: A Part-time Freelancer's Billable Hourly Rate

You're a part-time freelancer planning to add a 30% profit margin to your hourly burn rate of $50. Start by multiplying your hourly burn rate ($50) by 0.30 (i.e. 0.30 is 30% converted to a decimal number).

Step 01:

$$\$50 \times 0.30 = \$15$$

↑	↑	↑
Hourly Burn Rate	Profit Margin Percentage	Hourly Profit

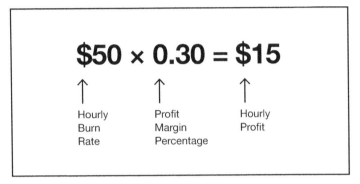

Next, take the $15 of hourly profit and add it back to your hourly burn rate, which equals a billable hourly rate of $65.

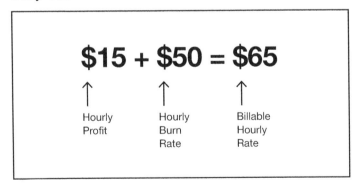

Step 02:

$$\$15 + \$50 = \$65$$

↑	↑	↑
Hourly Profit	Hourly Burn Rate	Billable Hourly Rate

Example 02: A Small Agency's Billable Hourly Rate

Let's look at another example as a small agency with a $72 hourly burn rate. If you have decided to markup your work by 40%, you would begin by multiplying your hourly burn rate by your profit margin percentage, 0.40 (i.e. 40% converted to a decimal number).

Step 01:

$$\$72 \times 0.40 = \$28.80$$

↑ Hourly Burn Rate — ↑ Profit Margin Percentage — ↑ Hourly Profit

As with the previous example, you would then add your hourly profit back to your hourly burn rate to calculate your billable hourly rate, $100.80.

Step 02:

$$\$28.80 + \$72 = \$100.80$$

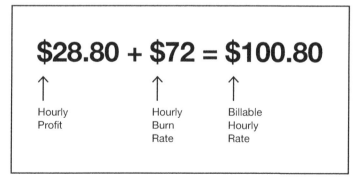

↑ Hourly Profit — ↑ Hourly Burn Rate — ↑ Billable Hourly Rate

Following the previously mentioned rule to always round up, **I recommend rounding billable hourly rates up to the nearest $5 increment**. In this case, you would round the billable hourly rate to $105 to err on the side of more profit, rather than less.

$105	Billable Hourly Rate (Rounded Up)

Example 03: A Full-time Freelancer's Billable Hourly Rate

Here is one final example as full-time freelancer with an hourly burn rate of $80. Since you have a lot of experience and produce high quality work, you have decided to add 75% profit to your rate (i.e. 0.75 is 75% converted to a decimal number).

Step 01:

$$\$80 \times 0.75 = \$60$$

$80	0.75	$60
↑ Hourly Burn Rate	↑ Profit Margin Percentage	↑ Hourly Profit

Then, as with the other examples, you would add your $60 hourly profit back to your hourly rate of $80 to yield $140. This billable hourly rate is already conveniently calculated to a $5 increment, so there is no need to round it further.

Step 02:

$60 + $80 = $140

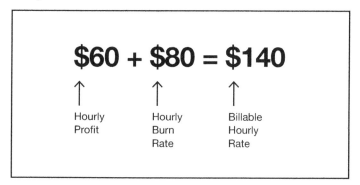

↑	↑	↑
Hourly Profit	Hourly Burn Rate	Billable Hourly Rate

A Final Warning

Now that you know how to calculate and understand your billable hourly rate, I want to reiterate how critical it is to use this in moderation. Every project that can be bid at a fixed price, should be. If your client asks you what your hourly rate is, simply respond by saying, "We have found that working on projects with a fixed bid is better for us and our clients. With a fixed bid, we all agree on the price before we start the project. We really only charge by the hour for things like website maintenance and minor content updates. When we do those types of things we charge $XXX per hour."

Billing by the hour is the least profitable way to price your work because it eliminates the value of the work you produce and penalizes you for working quickly.

Billable Hourly Rate Worksheet

Calculating Your Billable Hourly Rate

Step 01:

Decide how much profit to include in your billable hourly rate. This should be a percentage number that we will use in Step 02 to calculate an hourly profit.

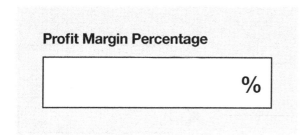

Profit Margin Percentage

%

Step 02:

Calculate your hourly burn rate using one of the worksheets provided in chapter one (pgs. 9-41). Then, multiply your hourly burn rate by the profit margin percentage you selected in Step 01. This calculation will yield your hourly profit.

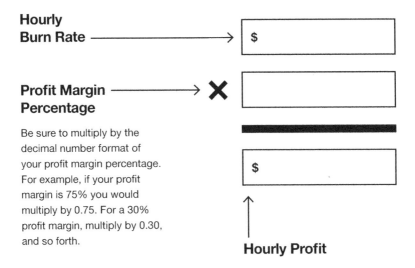

Hourly Burn Rate → $

Profit Margin Percentage → ×

Be sure to multiply by the decimal number format of your profit margin percentage. For example, if your profit margin is 75% you would multiply by 0.75. For a 30% profit margin, multiply by 0.30, and so forth.

$

Hourly Profit

Step 03:

Add the hourly profit calculated in Step 02 back to your hourly burn rate to yield your billable hourly rate.

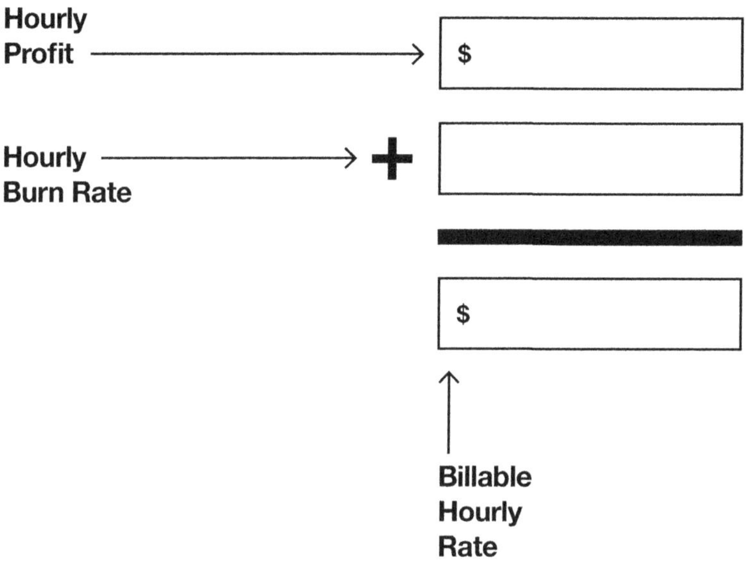

Round up your billable hourly rate to the nearest $5 increment. For example, if your calculation yielded a $103 billable hourly rate, you would round your final rate to $105. (As a reminder, always round up, even if math rules say you should round down. It is better to err on the side of more profit, rather than less.)

Billable Hourly Rate

$

09

CHAPTER 09

Pricing Presentation Strategies

Now that you've done all this work to understand your pricing numbers, we should probably discuss some best practices for presenting them to your clients.

There is no shortage of pricing tips, tricks, and strategies that have been studied and documented. In this chapter, I'll show you a handful of helpful ideas that apply to the type of sales initiatives we face as creative professionals.

Don't Just Email Pricing Numbers, Present Them

Before exploring some of these presentation strategies, I want to make it clear that you should always present your pricing numbers to the client. Don't just email a proposal and cross your fingers. The professional approach is to discuss your proposal and deliver your pricing numbers in person (a video chat or phone call are the next best options). This approach provides you have an opportunity for salesmanship, resolving concerns and inspiring them to choose to work with you on the project.

Commas and Pricing

There's a theory in the psychology of pricing, that the placement of commas in prices changes how we say the number. When we see the number $1599, we read it as "fifteen ninety nine," five syllables. In contrast, $1,599 would be read as "one thousand five hundred ninety nine," nine syllables. Numbers with commas are sub-consciously perceived as larger. *(Comma N' cents in pricing: The effects of auditory representation encoding on price magnitude perceptions, Keith Coulter, Pilsik Choi and Kent B. Monroe, Journal Of Consumer Psychology, 2012)*

Try reading the numbers in the grid below. Do you read "thirteen fifty" on line one in the first column? Does your brain want to say "one thousand three hundred and fifty" in column two? Which number sounds bigger to you?

Do This	Don't Do This
$1350	$1,350
$4500	$4,500
$9500	$9,500
$15,250	$15250
$34,750	$34750
$125,750	$125750

If you choose to follow this style of price formatting, I only recommend that you omit commas for prices below $10,000 due to legibility challenges. Anything larger than $10,000 is difficult to visually digest (e.g. $125750 vs. $125,750). Can you see the difference?

When presenting prices to our clients, we can use or omit commas to make our price seem as small and legible as possible.

Itemize Prices by Phases, Not Deliverables

When I started my design agency in 2002, I was a moderately accomplished designer, but a very novice businessman. I had never learned how to craft a proposal, price a project, invoice a client, or any other important business practices. As a result, I made mistakes that cost me money. One of the mistakes I made was the manner in which I proposed project prices.

In my early years, I operated my business under the assumption it was easier for a client to agree to a lump sum price if they could see how we arrived at the price. With this perspective, when a client presented me with a scope of work, I would respond with a proposal breaking down the deliverables with a line-item price per deliverable.

My logic was that the client would be more apt to sign-off on the lump sum price if they could see the smaller numbers that added up to it.

For example, if a client was requesting a logo design, business cards, and a letterhead, I would gauge how much I "felt" I should charge for the work and propose a price for each item. If I decided to charge $1,900 for the project, I would breakout my price in a manner like this:

Deliverable	Budget
Logo Design	$900
Business Card Design	$500
Letterhead Design	$500
TOTAL	$1900

Well, it didn't take me long to realize this strategy was flawed as it backfired on me over and over again. Inevitably, the client would see the line-item prices and say, "Thank you for the proposal, we have decided not to do the letterhead design and to go with just the logo and business cards for $1,400."

I realized when analyzing the price, my client's inner dialogue would likely be something like this, "Ok, $900 for the logo. We definitely need that. Hmmm...the business cards are $500, well,I we have to have those. $500 for the letterhead? That's a bit expensive for just a letterhead we will rarely use. We can live without the letterhead and do this project cheaper."

After a few financial losses relating directly to this flawed strategy, I adapted. Following the same objective of breaking down a high ticket item into more palatable prices, I began creating line-item prices for elements the client could not cut out of the project. Rather than breaking down the price by deliverables, I would break down the price by project phases. Let's look at how this is done using the same scope of work for a logo, business card design, and letterhead.

Production Phase	Budget
Phase 01: Initial Design Concepts	$700
Phase 02: Design Refinements	$700
Phase 03: Prepress File Preparation	$500
TOTAL	$1900

The first phase would be "Initial Design Concepts." This phase would include the initial comp ideas for the logo and show examples of how the logo concepts could transition into business card and letterhead designs. A client looking at this phase could not say, "We decided to wait on the initial design concepts and do that later." This is a phase that cannot be removed.

The next phase would be something like "Design Refinements." I would explain in my proposal this phase included taking one of the logo concepts and refining it into a final logo design, along with the business cards and letterhead. Again, the client could not remove this item.

After that phase, I might include a phase called "Prepress File Preparation." This is another item that cannot be extracted by the client. Of course, they will need and want press ready files!

This approach changes the client's inner dialogue to sound something like, "Hmmm...initial design concepts are $700, that sounds about right. Of course we need design refinements for $700. The final prepress prep is only $500, that's cheaper than I thought it would be. I guess $1,900 is a good price. I see how they arrived at that number."

*

Itemize your prices by project phases, not by deliverables.

Clients tend to agree on a bigger total price tag when they see how you arrived at the price; however, make sure your price breakdown only includes line-items not easily omitted from the project.

Use Font Sizes Wisely

As a designer, you create visual solutions to communicate effectively to a target audience. When it comes to proposal documents, we should use our best design strategies to communicate project prices to our clients. One of these tactics includes using font sizes to our advantage.

Our brains are conditioned to correlate the visual size of a number with the numeric size. Keith S. Coulter from Clark University and Robin A. Coulter from the University of Connecticut performed an interesting study supporting this correlation as documented in their 2005 article, *"Size Does Matter: The Effects of Magnitude Representation Congruency on Price Perceptions and Purchase Likelihood" (Journal of Consumer Psychology)*.

If you want your number to appear small, use a small font; if you want your number to appear large, use a large font. When presenting project pricing to our clients, we can use this technique to make our prices seem smaller and our discounts seem larger.

Does the price on the left seem more expensive than the price on the right?

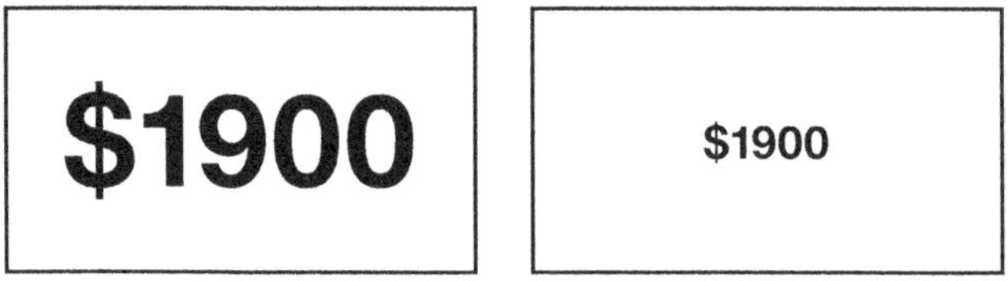

Designers have a tendency to emphasize the visual total because it creates a focal point on the page. I made this mistake for many years because the design looked better this way:

Production Phase	Budget
Phase 01: Initial Design Concepts	$700
Phase 02: Design Refinements	$700
Phase 03: Prepress File Preparation	$500
TOTAL	**$1900**

The larger font seems heavy to the client. But let's not get carried away and play games by making the total project price super small either, trying to de-emphasize its numerical value as seen below.

Production Phase	Budget
Phase 01: Initial Design Concepts	**$700**
Phase 02: Design Refinements	**$700**
Phase 03: Prepress File Preparation	**$500**
TOTAL	$1900

My recommendation is to use the same font size and weight for each of the line-items in your pricing breakdown, including the total project price, like this:

Production Phase	Budget
Phase 01: Initial Design Concepts	$700
Phase 02: Design Refinements	$700
Phase 03: Prepress File Preparation	$500
TOTAL	$1900

Solution First and Price Second

The order in which we present information in our proposals has a huge impact on the client's decision-making process. There is a legitimate, psychological reason for presenting your price last.

The sequence of price and product information has an influence on consumer decision-making. When the price is presented first, people base their purchase decision on economic value, according to a 2015 study. *(Cost Conscious? The Neural and Behavioral Impact of Price Primacy on Decision Making, Uma R. Karmarkar, Baba Shiv, and Brian Knutson, Journal of Marketing Research, 2015)*

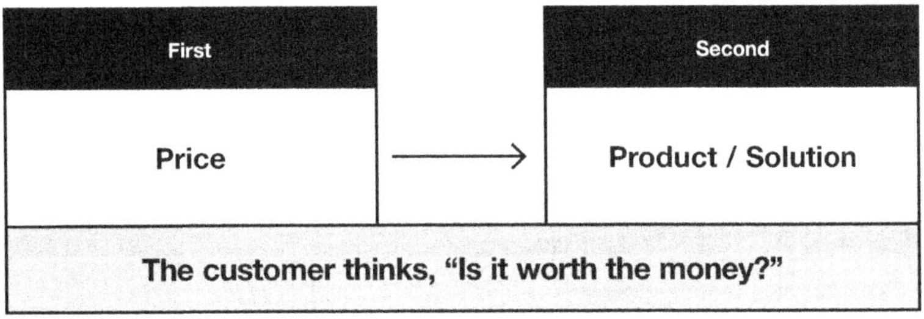

Whereas, if the product is presented first, people make purchasing decisions based on the quality of the product.

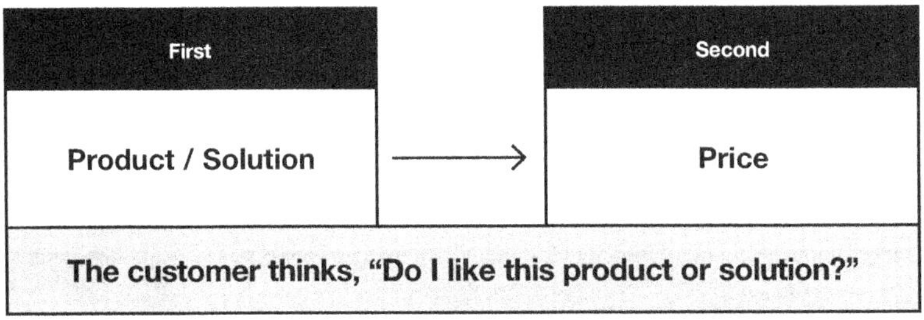

Walk your client through your proposed solution first. Explain the work you will do and how you will solve their business problems through your design solution. Show them examples of how you have successfully done this in the past. Then, after they are sitting back in their chair thinking to themselves, "I like this solution," you present your price.

Show Your Discounts

Every designer has a time or two when they discount their typical project rate in an effort to land a client. Sometimes, there is a project you really want to work on, but the budget is lower than you had hoped. Other times, you may discount your prices to hook a client into a longer term relationship. Finally, if we are being completely transparent, there are times when you discount your rates to help your entrepreneurial sister-in-law get her business started.

We discussed how to price your projects in these types of scenarios earlier in this book, and as long as you are comfortable with your profitability, there is nothing fundamentally wrong with discounting your pricing to perform work for a client. The problem occurs when we don't show the discounts to our clients in our project agreement. Show your discounts!

Let's assume you are building a website for a new client. The client's budget is $12,500. You usually charge $14,500 for this type of project, but you are comfortable doing the work for their budget because you know your numbers and your production cost is $9,500. You are excited about the work because it is a cool company with a bright future that you want to help create.

A typical freelancer or agency will incorrectly present only the discounted pricing as in the example below. (You'll see that I have broken down the project into phases as previously instructed.)

Production Phase	Budget
Phase 01: Content Strategy	$1500
Phase 02: User Experience Design (UX)	$3000
Phase 03: User Interface Design (UI)	$3500
Phase 04: Development & QA Testing	$5000
TOTAL	$12,500

When you do it this way, you have just taught your client that you typically charge $12,500 for this type of project and they have it in writing. When your client's coworker, Joan (who works in a different department), asks how much the site cost, she is told $12,500. Joan then tells her boss, Sally, who needs a website for her department. Sally calls you expecting a $12,500 site. By the way, Sally also told her husband your pricing. He works for a bank that is looking for a new digital agency and calls you expecting a $12,500 website. You are now stuck in a perpetually discounted rate for website design and development.

A better method is to always show your discounts. If your typical price for this type of project is $14,500, but you are willing to do the work for $12,500, you must show the discount as a line-item in the pricing grid of your proposal.

Production Phase	Budget
Phase 01: Content Strategy	$1500
Phase 02: User Experience Design (UX)	$3500
Phase 03: User Interface Design (UI)	$4000
Phase 04: Development & QA Testing	$5500
TOTAL	$14,500
End of Year Discount	–$2000
DISCOUNTED TOTAL	$12,500

This method allows you to provide the client with a discounted rate, while mitigating the risk of perpetual future discount expectations from this same client or others.

What ways can you show a line-item discount? You could offer a "package discount" for engagement with a variety of deliverables. A "new client discount" is always a safe bet. If you are offering a discounted rate to a client, be creative in how you want to phrase it to your customer. Just make sure you show it in your price breakdown.

10

CHAPTER 10

Conclusion & Pricing Rules

When I started my freelance career, that grew into my agency, I had no understanding of any of the calculations and strategies that I have taught in this book. Trial and error, both successful and unsuccessful, taught me to develop these systems and strategies. I have shared with you every thought process I could to help you understand the psychology behind pricing your creative work.

With a firm understanding of your production cost, a clear picture of the market value of your work, along with the tactics necessary to extract the client's budget, you are now equipped to confidently choose the right price for any project. Over time you will develop a sixth sense for bidding projects, which can empower you to know the right price without all the calculations. Until then, take your time, analyze the variables, and appropriately price your work for each scenario. These systems and strategies will allow you to win more bids and earn more profit.

In conclusion, here a few key takeaways and rules you can adopt in your business. These guidelines can provide you with a foundation for decision-making when things get crazy in your career as a creative professional.

Pricing Rules & Reminders for Graphic Designers

01

Always discuss money with confidence.

Take time to calculate your numbers and always discuss money with confidence. If a client senses you lack confidence in your pricing, they will lose confidence in you.

02

Never feel bad about earning a sizable profit on a project.

You are in business to make a profit. Not every project is going to be fun, but every project should be profitable. For every project with a sizable profit, there will inevitably be a low profit project to balance it out.

03

Never take on a project that is guaranteed to be unprofitable.

Never price a project lower than your cost to produce it. Take the time to calculate your production cost and use that number as your guide to profitability.

04

Don’t play number games.

Don’t play games by pricing your projects at $999 or $5,999 or any “left-digit effect” number. Round your prices to the nearest whole numbers by $25, $50, and $250 increments. The bigger the price, the bigger the rounded increment.

05

Every project that can be bid at a fixed price, should be.

Fixed bid pricing allows you to take advantage of market value and rewards you for working quickly. You should only charge your client by the hour for small change requests and maintenance items.

06

Itemize project prices by phases, not deliverables.

Always break down project prices by phases in your proposals, not deliverables. Each phase should be something the client cannot pull from the project in an effort to reduce the budget.

07

Never tell your client how much profit you are making on a project.

The size of your profitability is irrelevant to your client. Do not share it.

08

Never tell your client how many hours you have allocated to a fixed bid project.

After you have agreed upon price, the number of hours it takes you to complete the work is irrelevant. You only track and calculate hours to ensure profitability, not to price your work by the hour.

About the Author

Michael Janda is an award-winning creative director, designer, agency owner, and author. In 2002, he founded the creative agency Riser, which provided design and development services for clients that included Disney, Google, Warner Bros., Fox, NBC, ABC, National Geographic, and many other high-profile brands. Following 13 successful years, Michael sold his agency in 2015. He now spends his time writing, speaking, and mentoring to help freelancers and agencies navigate the complex world of design.

Prior to founding his agency, Michael served as a Senior Creative Director at Fox Studios where he managed the design, editorial, and development teams for the Fox Kids and Fox Family brands.

Michael's book, *Burn Your Portfolio: Stuff They Don't Teach You In Design School But Should*, was published in 2013 and has been one of the top-selling design industry books since its release.

His work, book, and agency have received awards and recognition from Inc. 5000, FWA, Awwwards, HOW Magazine, Print Magazine, Ad News Magazine, Huffington Post, Promax/BDA, AIGA 100, Addy Awards, Webby Awards, and BusinessQ Magazine.

Michael lives in Utah with his wife of more than 20 years, their three sons, and a collection of more than 100 bobbleheads.

michaeljanda.com

Let’s connect!

@morejanda

Share this book!

#psychopricing

Made in the USA
Monee, IL
26 November 2019

17439066R00115